Helion & Company Limited
Unit 8 Amherst Business Centre
Budbrooke Road
Warwick
CV34 5WE
England
Tel. 01926 499 619
Email: info@helion.co.uk
Website: www.helion.co.uk
Twitter: @helionbooks
Visit our blog http://blog.helion.co.uk/

Designed and typeset by Farr out Publications, Wokingham, Berkshire
Cover design by Paul Hewitt, Battlefield Design (www.battlefi eld-design.co.uk)

ISBN 978-1-914377-02-0

British Library Cataloguing-in-Publication Data
A catalogue record for this book is available from the British Library

We always welcome receiving book proposals from prospective authors.

CONTENTS

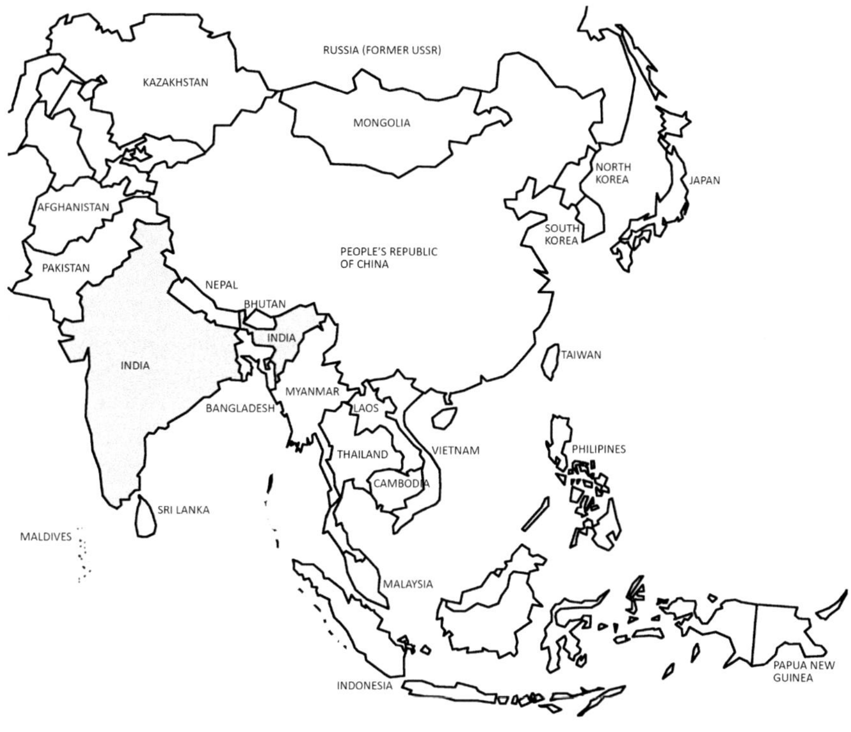

Note: In order to simplify the use of this book, all names, locations and geographic designations are as provided in *The Times World Atlas*, or other traditionally accepted major sources of reference, as of the time of described events.

LIST OF ABBREVIATIONS

AAC	Army Aviation Corps
APC	Armoured Personnel Carrier
ARDE	Armament Research and Development Establishment
ATGM	Anti-Tank Guided Missile
CO	Commanding Officer
FOC-in-C	Flag Officer Commanding in Chief
IAF	Indian Air Force
ICV	Infantry Combat Vehicle
IFG	Indian Field Gun
IMSF	Indian Marine Special Forces
INS	Indian Naval Ship
LTTE	Liberation Tigers of Tamil Eelam
MANPADS	Man Portable Air Defence System
MARCOS	Marine Commandos
MCF	Marine Commando Force
MDP	Maldivian Democratic Party
NSG	National Security Guards
NSS	National Security Service
Para	Paratroop Regiment
Para Cdo	Paratroop Commando
Para SF	Paratroop Regiment (Special Forces)
PFLP	Popular Front for the Liberation of Palestine
PLOTE	People's Liberation Organization of Tamil Eelam
RAW	Research and Analysis Wing
SAM	Surface to Air Missile
TELO	Tamil Eelam Liberation Organization
TULF	Tamil United Liberation Front

1
INTRODUCTION, THE MALDIVES AND SRI LANKA'S TAMIL INSURGENTS

Operation Cactus – A Summary and Its Significance

Operation Cactus was an Indian response to the 1988 Maldives coup d'état. The coup was an attempt by a group of Maldivians led by businessman Abdullah Luthufi which enlisted armed mercenaries of a Tamil secessionist organisation from Sri Lanka – the People's Liberation Organisation of Tamil Eelam (PLOTE). They sought to overthrow the government in the island republic of Maldives and were inspired by the deeply flawed electoral process in the Maldives itself.

The coup d'état failed after the intervention of Indian paratroopers and Special Forces, who not only secured the Maldivian capital, Malé, but also eliminated the terrorist leaders of PLOTE. Upon realising their failure, the surviving members of the terrorist group hijacked a Maldivian freighter named the MV *Progress Light* and attempted to escape, probably back to Sri Lanka. After they fled, Indian ground forces called for naval assistance, and in a coordinated air and sea action, the Indian Navy intercepted and captured the mercenaries, who were brought to justice.

Two earlier attempts at insurrection had been made in the Maldives in 1980 and 1983. These attempted coups d'état against Maumoon Abdul Gayoom's presidency were not deemed to be sufficient by the plotters, but the third attempt in November 1988 was a much more serious affair, causing alarm in the international community.

As will be detailed below, the 1988 operation was well planned and involved about 80 armed PLOTE mercenaries who landed in the capital Malé, just before down, using speedboats deployed from a hijacked Sri Lankan freighter. Exploiting the Maldives' reputation as a holiday resort, an equal number of PLOTE operatives, disguised as tourists, had already infiltrated Malé some time earlier. The armed mercenaries were quickly able to gain control of the capital and such important installations as major government buildings, the airport, port and television and radio stations.[1]

However, their attempt to apprehend the president was thwarted when – while the mercenaries were moving towards the presidential palace where President Gayoom was residing with his family – the Maldivian National Security advisor escorted the president to the defence minister's home. The defence minister then escorted the president to a safe house, where they awaited assistance.[2]

Though the mercenaries had seized the presidential palace and managed to take the Maldivian education minister as hostage, President Gayoom was able to request military intervention, initially from Sri Lanka and Pakistan. However, both these states declined, citing a lack of military capability. The president then sought Singapore's intervention, but again Singapore declined, citing its own limitations.[3]

After that, Gayoom contacted the United States, but owing to the distance from their military base at Diego Garcia – some 1,000km – their intervention would take at least two days to reach the Maldives. The president, in desperation, then contacted the United Kingdom, which very pragmatically advised him to seek assistance from India. It was only then that President Gayoom made contact with the Indian government for assistance. As will be shown, India acted upon this request; after an emergency meeting was arranged at the Secretariat Building in New Delhi, India planned and launched its operation within 16 hours of receiving the request for assistance. It was short, sharp and, more importantly, successful.[4]

This operation – carried out at the last moment, with existing resources and conducted at a place many thousands of kilometres away from India – was a watershed for both India and the Maldives. It cemented India's place as a regional security provider and ensured that its close ties to the Maldives acquired an important military dimension, with Indian forces now always being deployed close to

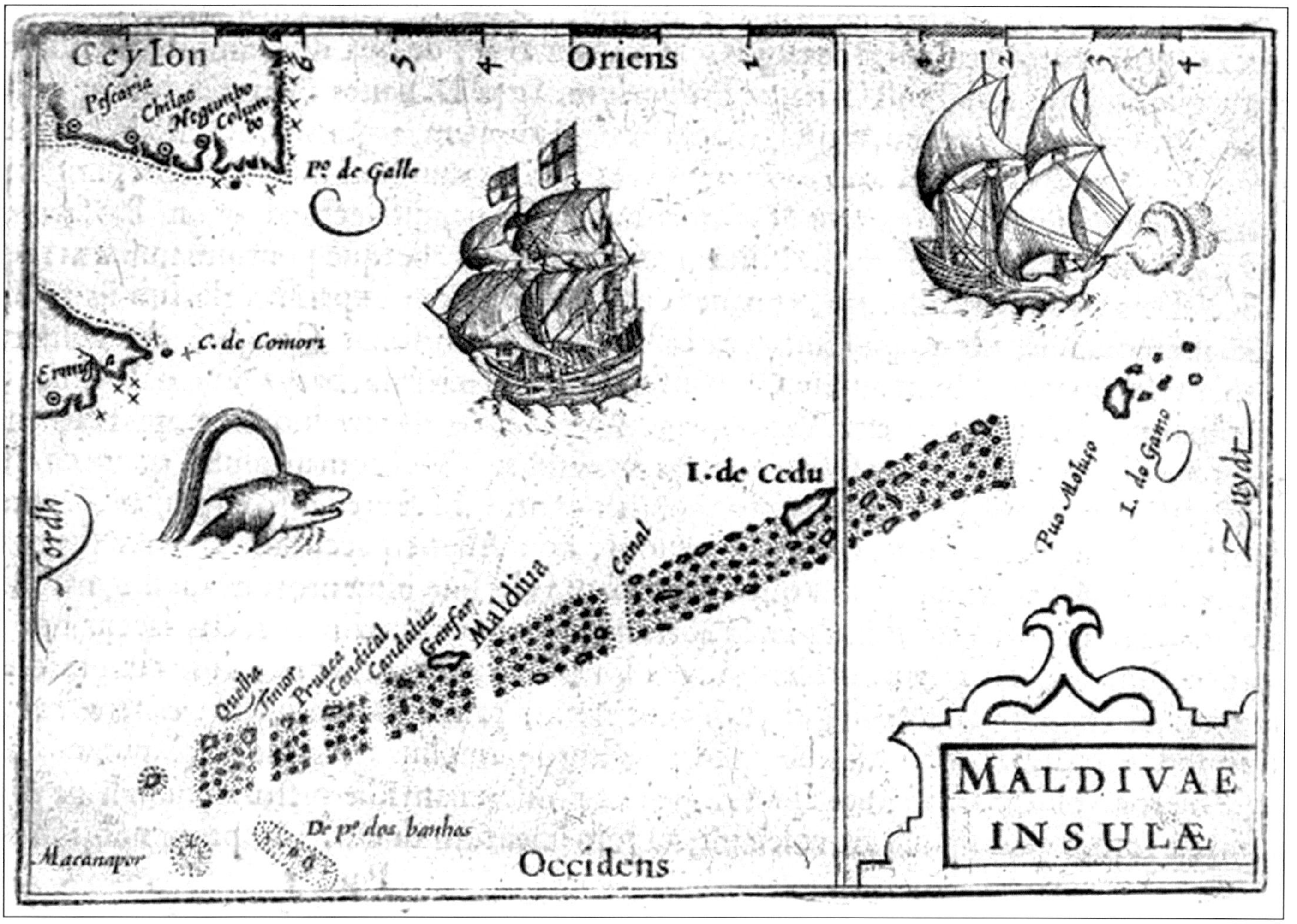

Bertius' map of Maldives, issued in Middelburg, Netherlands, in 1598. (Open source)

the Maldives on routine operations, but with the ability to intervene if needed.

The Maldives

The Republic of Maldives is a small archipelagic state in the Arabian Sea of the Indian Ocean. It lies southwest of Sri Lanka and India, about 700 kilometres (430 miles) from the Indian subcontinent's mainland. The chain consists of 26 atolls and stretches from Ihavandhippolhu Atoll in the north to Addu Atoll – which is near to the equator – in the south.[5]

Its territory spans roughly 298 square kilometres (115 square miles), and while tiny, the Maldives is one of the most geographically dispersed of the world's sovereign states. It is the smallest Asian country by both land area and population, which currently stands at a little over half a million people. Its capital city of Malé is the country's most populated city, and is traditionally called the King's Island, from where the ancient royal dynasties ruled because of its central location.

Geographically and geologically, the Maldives archipelago is located on the Chagos-Laccadive Ridge, a massive submarine mountain range in the Indian Ocean. It also forms what is termed a terrestrial ecoregion, in conjunction with the Chagos archipelago and India's Lakshadweep islands. It is a very low-lying country with no mountain ranges; the country has an average ground-level elevation of 1.5 metres (4ft 11in) above sea level. Its highest natural point is also one of the lowest in the world, at just 5.1 metres (17ft) above sea level.[6]

The main religion of its population, Islam, reached the Maldivian archipelago in the twelfth century. The archipelago was thereafter consolidated as a sultanate, and exploiting its exceptional geographic location, it developed strong commercial and cultural ties with Asia and Africa, as well as with the Arab world.

Of the 1,190 islands in the Maldives archipelago, only 198 are inhabited. Even on these islands, the population is scattered among them, with the greatest concentration on the capital island, Malé. There are severe limitations on drinkable water and arable land, which presents challenges to not only residents of the Maldives but also the sustainability of its tourist economy.

Early History

Legends and history often intersect in respect of the age of the Maldives, which is an old nation, or at least an old entity – dating back some 2,500 years, according to the legends of the Allama Ahmed Shihabuddine (Allama Shihab al-Din) of Meedhoo in Addu Atoll. He claims, in the book *Kitāb fi āthār Mīdhu al-qādimah* (كتاب في اثار ميذو القديمة; *On the Ancient Ruins of Meedhoo*), written in the seventeenth century in Arabic, that the first settlers of the Maldives were people known as Dheyvis. They allegedly came from the Kalibanga in India. This was purportedly before the Maurya Emperor Ashoka's rule from in 269–232 BC.[7]

A strong underlying layer of southern Indian Dravidian population and culture survives in Maldivian society, with some considerable evidence of both Tamil and Malayalam features in the language of the Maldives. This is also evident from any study of place names, kinship terms, poetry, dance and religious beliefs prior to

Islam. South Indian Malabari seafaring culture was instrumental in the settlement of the islands by Malayali seafarers, and the Maldives were no exception.[8]

As was the norm, and as part of the gradual building of the English and French colonial empires, from the mid-sixteenth century onwards the region came under the increasing influence of various European powers. This culminated with the Maldives becoming a British protectorate in 1887.

It is interesting to note that the Maldives has remained an independent nation throughout its recorded history, save for a brief spell of Portuguese occupation in the middle of the sixteenth century. Between 1887 and 1965, the country was a British protectorate while retaining full internal sovereignty. Upon its independence in 1965, the Maldives joined the United Nations on 20 September of that year.

A presidential republic was established in 1968, with an elected People's Majlis. The ensuing decades have seen political instability, efforts at democratic reform and environmental challenges posed by climate change.

Politics

The political history of the Maldives in the twentieth and twenty-first centuries is interesting as a study in its own right. Following the death of Sultan Abdul Majeed Didi on 21 February 1952, the members of the country's parliament, the People's Majlis, chose Mohamed Amin Didi to be the next Sultan, but in an act of political sagacity, he stated that 'for the sake of the people of Maldives I will not accept the crown and the throne'.

Thereafter, the People's Majlis voted on 13 April the same year to form a commission, with Amin Didi as its chairman, to determine the country's future governance structure and to create a new system of both electoral administration and constitutional governance. The commission was highly distinguished and qualified, and included the noted scholar Famuladeyri Kaleygefan, Chief Justice Abdullah Jalaludeen, Majlis Speaker Malim Moosa Mafaiy Kilegefan, Deputy Vazirul-Auzam Ibrahim Mohamed Didi, Kolhumadulu Atoll MP Ibrahim Shihab, Galolhu MP Bucha Hassan Kaleygefan and Faadhippolhu Atoll chief Kaannaa Kaleygefan.

On 16 April 1952, after the short operation of the group, the People's Majlis affirmed the commission's decision to form a republic and to hold a referendum on a new constitution for the islands. The results of this referendum led to the Maldives becoming a republic, with Amin Didi as the first elected president, having abolished the 812-year-old sultanate. Though as a president he is remembered as a reformer of the education system and a promoter of women's rights, while he was in Ceylon to undergo medical treatment, a revolt led by his deputy, Velaanaagey Ibrahim Didi, was successfully conducted. When President Amin Didi returned, he was confined to Dhoonidhoo Island. Although he escaped to Malé and tried to take control of the city of Bandeyrige, he was beaten by an angry mob and died soon after.

After the fall of Amin Didi's presidency, a referendum was held and 98 percent of the people voted in favour of a restoration of the monarchy, so the country was once again declared a sultanate. A new People's Majlis was elected, after its dissolution following the revolt. Its members decided to take a secret vote to elect a sultan, leading to Prince Mohammed Fareed Didi being elected as the 84th Sultan of the Maldives in 1954. The new sultan's first prime minister was Ehgamugey Ibrahim Ali Didi (later Ibrahim Faamuladheyri Kilegefaan). However, on 11 December 1957, the prime minister was forced to resign and Velaanagey Ibrahim Nasir was elected to replace him the following day.

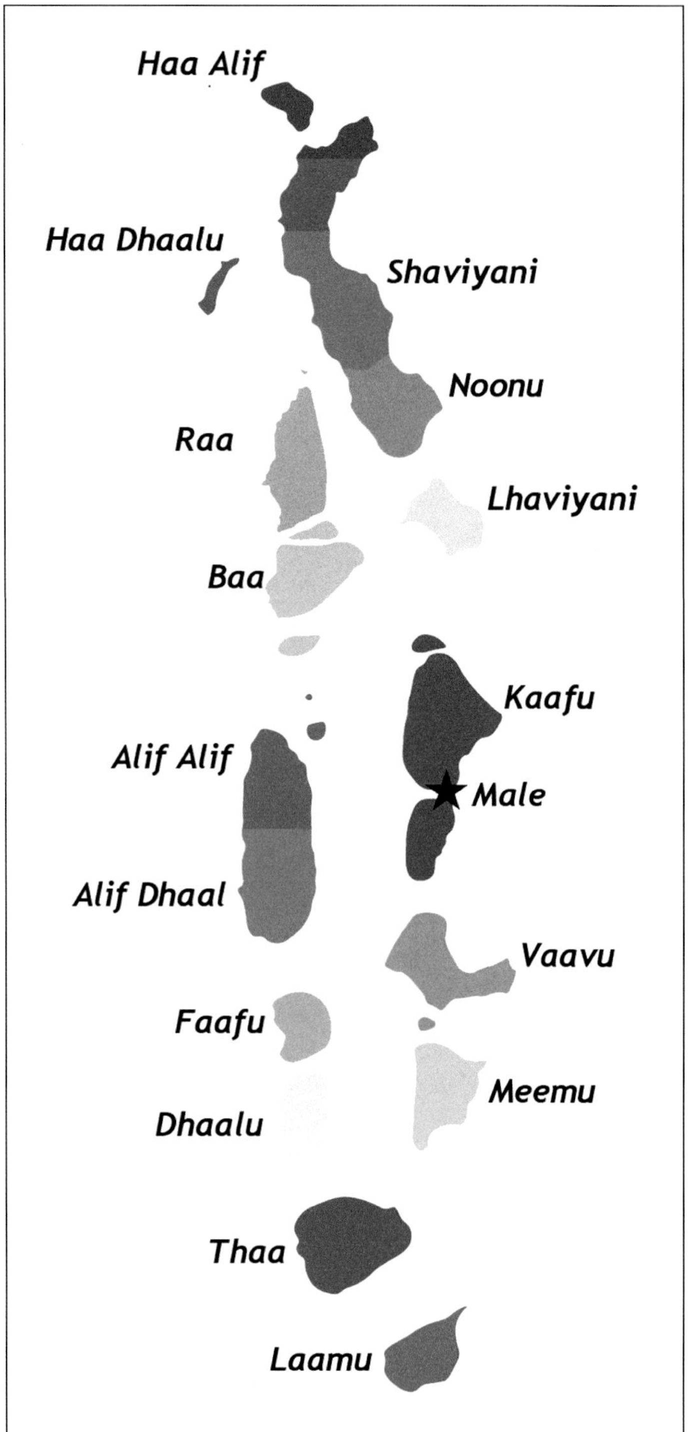

The islands of the Maldives. (Map by Tom Cooper)

It should be noted that the United Kingdom maintained a large military presence in the Maldives until 1976. In 1956, the UK sought and obtained permission to re-establish its wartime RAF Gan airfield in the southernmost Addu Atoll, which enabled the employment of hundreds of locals. The Maldives granted the British a 100-year lease on the base at Gan that required them to pay £2,000 a year, plus a 100-year lease for some 440,000 square metres on Hitaddu for radio installations. These bases served as a staging post for British military flights to the Far East and Australia, replacing RAF Mauripur in Pakistan, which had been vacated earlier that year.[9]

In 1957, the islands' relationship with Britain began to change. The new prime minister, Ibrahim Nasir, called for a review of the agreement with a view to shortening the lease and increasing the annual payment. Subsequently, there was a challenge in 1959 from

The withdrawal of the last British troops from the British military airfield staging post at Gan, on 29 March 1976: ever since then, this date is celebrated as the independence day of the Maldives. (Foreign Service Institute of Maldives)

a local secessionist movement in the three southernmost atolls that benefited economically from the British presence on Gan.[10]

This led to the formation of an independent state, the United Suvadive Republic, with Abdullah Afif as president, Hithadhoo as its capital and a small population of 20,000 inhabitants scattered over Huvadu, Addu and Fua Mulaku. Pleas for recognition by Britain came to nought as the British, while not unsympathetic to requests for increased payments, were not keen on a secession movement in the Maldives. In the end, the point was moot as the base was closed in 1976 as part of a scaling down of global commitments, with the British withdrawal of permanently stationed forces 'East of Suez', initiated by the Labour government of Harold Wilson, which led to the British military ending their presence in southern Asia.[11]

Following independence in 1965 and the end of the sultanate, a referendum was held to determine the Maldives' constitutional fate. The 1968 referendum approved a constitution making the Maldives a republic, with the attendant executive, legislative and judicial branches of government. This constitution was amended in 1970, 1972, 1975 and 1997 and again in 2008.

As might be expected, Ibrahim Nasir, who was prime minister under the pre-1968 sultanate, became president and held the office from 1968–1978. After his second term, he was succeeded by Maumoon Abdul Gayoom, who was elected president in 1978 and re-elected in 1983, 1988, 1993, 1998 and 2003. At the end of his presidency in 2008, Gayoom was the longest-serving leader in Asia, but he remains a controversial figure.

Gayoom's rise began as Ibrahim Nasir's second term was coming to an end, and when he decided not to seek re-election in June 1978, the Citizen's Majlis was asked to nominate a presidential candidate as required under the country's then constitution. Despite his refusal to seek re-election, there were 45 votes for Nasir, with only three for Abdul Gayoom. This led to another ballot being called on 16 June, at which Gayoom received 27 votes and allowed himself to be declared the sole candidate.[12]

In elections held five months later, Gayoom was elected the new President of the Maldives, with 92.96 percent of the votes cast. Subsequently, in a 1983 referendum, he was re-elected on 30 September for a second term, polling a record 95.6 percent, and thereafter on 23 September 1988, he was re-elected for a third term with an even larger 96.4 percent of the popular vote – just a few months before the coup.

Even after the events of 1988, on 1 October 1993, Gayoom was elected for an astonishing fourth term with 92.76 percent of the popular vote. This was followed on 16 October 1998 by the start of an unprecedented fifth term of office, this time with 90.9 percent of the vote. Gayoom was re-elected for a sixth and final five-year term in October 2003 after receiving 90.28 percent of the vote. In all cases, he was the sole candidate, having been nominated by the Majlis and having in every possible way dissuaded rival candidates. In many ways, he was effectively an elected despot.[13]

In this regard, Gayoom was very much following in the vein of Nasir, widely criticised for being an authoritarian leader and for internal political repression.

As has often been the case throughout recorded history, upon taking office Gayoom promised liberal reforms but spent much of his time and effort in consolidating his personal grip on power. This he did to an extreme extent, carefully skirting the boundaries of becoming an outright tyrant. In one of his first moves, he replaced the leaders of the security forces – which were kept very modest – with loyal supporters.

He also invested his brother, Abdulla Hameed, as chief governor of all the provinces, thereby ensuring administrative compliance. The nepotism continued when he placed a brother-in-law as the head of security and trade, while as control of the media was seen as vital, he put another brother-in-law in charge of the nation's only

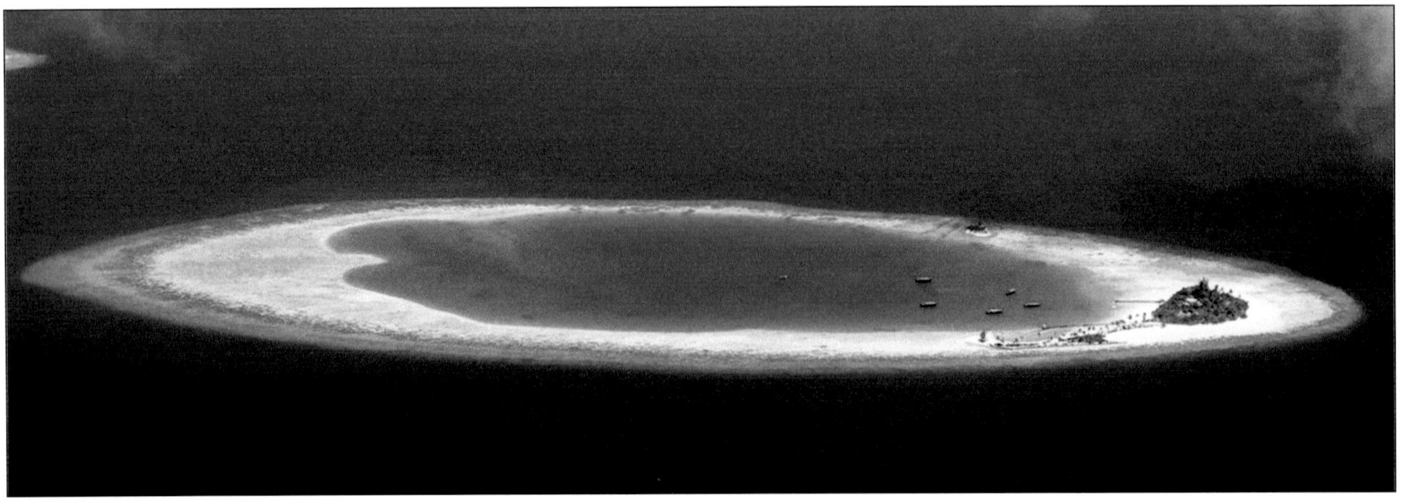

One of the thousands of minor atolls in the Maldives archipelago. (Maldives Ministry of Environment and Energy)

President Maumoon Abdul Gayoom with Prime Minister of India, Rajiv Gandhi. (Indian Government, official release)

media, a radio station. He then gave the latter the task of developing a rudimentary TV station and turning this into an instrument of state propaganda.[14]

This set an unhealthy trend for the next 20 years, as President Gayoom steadily built barriers to shield his powers while aggressively undermining the growing and increasingly assertive Maldivian civil society. This culminated in 1997 when the Special Majlis, a select group of parliamentarians, produced a new constitution which served to significantly enhance Gyoom's executive powers. Not surprisingly, even this had shades of nepotism, as Gayoom's brother, Abdulla Hameed, guided the Special Majlis. This served to effectively entrench Gayoom in office long enough to become one of Asia's longest standing 'elected' dictators, a position which he held until 2008.

For the 30 years of his rule, President Gayoom refused to acknowledge any political parties as having legitimacy. He vacuously stated that the existence of opposition parties wound not be in the best interests of the 'homogeneous nature of Maldivian society'.

Despite these challenges, the Maldivian Democratic Party (MDP) was formed in Britain in 2001 and began organising itself. The MDP, with little political experience, relied on the support of like-minded citizens, or at least those in favour of parliamentary democracy. The MDP would play a key role unifying and organising the various opposition groups into a force able to defeat Gayoom in the 2008 elections.[15]

The Maldives continues to have relatively weak democratic and judicial structures, with subsequent presidents being prone to abusing their offices. The presidency of Abdullah Yameen, who governed between 2013 and 2018, was particularly notorious for his subversion of the judiciary, the incarceration of political opponents and his casual use of states of emergency to further suppress civil liberties in the country.

The inability of the country's parliamentary and judicial arms to stop this blatant abuse of power by an elected official is particularly noteworthy, as it shows that the Maldives are yet to become a strong and sustainable democracy.

Internationally, the Maldives became a founding member of the South Asian Association for Regional Cooperation (SAARC) and, as previously noted, it is also a member of the United Nations. In addition, it is a member the Commonwealth of Nations, the Organisation of Islamic Cooperation and the Non-Aligned Movement.

The Maldives was a member of the Commonwealth from July 1982 until withdrawing from the organisation in October 2016. This was in response to concerns raised by other Commonwealth members of its increasing internal repression and human rights abuses, plus its subversion of elections and being widely seen as a failing democracy. Subsequently, and following a change of government, the Maldives rejoined the Commonwealth on 1 February 2020.

Economy

The economy of the Maldives is based on the principal activities of tourism, fishing and shipping. It is a mixed economy that has delivered a remarkably high level of development, and its per capita income is the highest in the South Asian region.

In no small part, this is due to tourism, which is the largest industry in the Maldives, accounting for 28 percent of GDP and more than 60 percent of the Maldives' foreign exchange receipts. Indeed, tourism enabled the country's GDP per capita to increase by 265 percent in the 1980s and a further 115 percent in the 1990s. Unsurprisingly, some 90 percent of government tax revenue flows in from import duties and tourism-related taxes.

Monetary receipts from the tourism sector have enabled the development of the country's infrastructure throughout all the islands in the Maldives archipelago. With revenue mainly dependent on the tourism industry and its complementary tertiary sectors – transport, distribution, real estate, construction and government – taxes on the tourist industry have been ploughed into infrastructure, and in a positive development have been used to improve technology in the agricultural sector.

A typical scene from Dharu Maarukeytu – one of many ports around the archipelago, used for exchange of all sorts of goods – in the 1970s. (Mark Lepko Collection)

Sun, blue sky and countless and endless beaches with soft sand and clear water have been attracting tourists to the Maldives for decades. Indeed, tourism remains the primary branch of the local economy. (Maldives Ministry of Environment and Energy)

Despite their natural beauty, tourism in the Maldives had a rocky start and only really began in 1972. A United Nations mission on development which visited the Maldives in the 1960s apparently did not recommend tourism as a major industry, making the seemingly bizarre claim that that the islands were not suitable.

However, since the coming of the first tourist resort to the Maldives in 1972, tourism has flourished. From the arrival of the first group of tourists in February 1972, resort tourism in Maldives has skyrocketed. It started with just two resorts with a capacity of about 280 beds, the Kurumba Island Resort being the first resort opened in Maldives, followed by Bandos Island Resort. There are now no fewer than 132 resorts located in most of the different atolls constituting the Republic of Maldives.[16]

Not surprisingly, over the last five decades, the number of tourists visiting the Maldives has risen exponentially. Privately owned guesthouses established through a change in regulations now officially allow tourists to stay among the local population, rather than on privately owned resort islands, thus enhancing the tourist experience as well as enabling individuals to share in the tourist business as entrepreneurs.[17]

Other notable industries around the islands include fishing and agriculture. They have been enabled by investment ploughed into them from the tourism sector, while the waters of the Indian Ocean provide a strong base for commercial and recreational fishing. The agricultural sector is small, limited by the country's size, but it is nonetheless a part of the country's economy. The manufacturing sector, which contributes 18 percent of the Maldives' GDP, is based on garment production, mainly for export to the West and driven heavily by foreign investment, taking advantage of the liberal economy, low tariffs and favourable climate.

Social and Political Problems

During his presidency, as part of a promise to improve prosperity, Gayoom incrementally pushed the Maldivian economy to be based on luxury resort tourism. This inevitably led to a heavy degree of income disparity and issues with distribution. Workers in $5,000-per-night hotels received small recompense for their work. A scathing article in *The New Statesman*, written in 2008, quoted Tricia Barnett, director of an organisation called Tourism Concern that fights exploitation in global tourism. She stated: 'It is not paradise for anybody … Living conditions for most Maldivians are akin to those in sub-Saharan Africa. There has been no trickle down of the extraordinary amount of money being generated.'

Gayoom's personal wealth was astonishing, and he was not shy about flaunting it. This attracted attention from the Maldives' national auditor, which stated that Gayoom's personal spending was 'out of control'. Gayoom's named assets mentioned $9.5 million spent on a luxury yacht, and his spending also included $17 million to renovate the presidential palace and the purchase of 11 speedboats and 55 cars with government money. It was seen as particularly obscene for this kind of corruption to occur when 40 percent of ordinary Maldivians were living on roughly $1 per day.

Inevitably, this created ample scope for severe public discontent and grievances.[18]

Socially, the income inequality and rapid move towards urbanisation and economic inequality adversely impacted the traditional family structures and community frameworks and values that operated as both a social support network and a form of social security.

This laid a fertile groundwork for a dangerous combination of problems: destitution, crime, Islamic extremism and drug abuse.

While accurate statistics are inevitably difficult to get, some estimates have suggested that one in 10 Maldivians struggle with some form of substance abuse. In recent times, a United Nations Development Program study produced staggering estimates that 40 percent of Maldivian youths were using hard drugs. When consideration is given to the fact that some 60 percent of the population is under 25 years of age, the incidence of drug use is terrifying.[19]

As might be expected with a low-income, youth-heavy population in South Asia, the most popular drug and the one most widely used is a low-grade form of heroin that locals call 'Brown Sugar'. Social scientists further suggest that the country's capital – the densely populated island city of Malé – is not only the ideal environment for the spread of addiction, but also where users find it easy to addict due to their close proximity to other users.[20]

The Maldives, therefore, despite being undoubtedly one of the more prosperous countries in South Asia, has a peculiar blend of social problems, exacerbated by income inequality, the tourist industry and the ready availability of cheap and highly addictive narcotics. This has led to major concerns in recent times, such as a rising tide of Islamic fundamentalism, a persistent piracy problem and a seemingly intractable issue with sustaining democracy, with religious sentiment often being invoked to either support or denounce a political party, often at the behest of foreign powers with agendas entirely of their own.

Thus the Maldives were and are a remarkable country – small, somewhat isolated but very prosperous, with a very interesting socio-economic and political history. Its location in the Arabian Sea gives it a strategic importance which continues to grow. The fate of the Maldives is of concern to regional powers, and it was this that prompted the events of 1988 – both the coup and the Indian response that ended it.

The Politics of the Maldives and the Genesis of the Coup

Gayoom's 'election' in 1988 presented a cause for both opportunity and frustration to his critics. Allegations of the involvement of former President Ibrahim Nasir in the coup attempts of 1980 and 1983 remain unconfirmed, but the fact that Gayoom was elected by a landslide in 1988, with no opposition candidate, did his democratic credentials no good. This enabled opposition forces to consider their chances for ousting the president, However, there was no coherent plan for replacing him with a more democratic entity and nobody clearly articulated a move to multi-party democracy for the republic, which was not surprising considering that Nasir's administration was very authoritarian.

This trend of authoritarianism, sometimes legitimised through uncontested elections, was enabled by the compromising of the Majlis, or what passed for a parliament in the Maldives. That there was no independent constitutional authority capable of deterring such an abuse of process was to eventually have dire consequences for the Maldives as its political history evolved in the late twentieth and early twenty-first centuries.

In 1980, Ahmed Naseem, Nasir's brother-in-law and a former junior minister, became increasingly concerned that Gayoom's government was getting uncomfortably close to uncovering a large number of fiscal irregularities in the records of the former administration. Adding to his concerns was the investigation into the torture and murder of inmates in the country's Villingili prison in the 1970s, which implicated the minister of public safety under Nasir, one Abdul Hannan Haleem, in those abuses and further soured Naseem's feelings towards the Gayoom administration.[21] This led to the plotting and launching of the first coup attempt against Gayoom, which set in motion a trend of periodic attempts to depose him, all of which would be unsuccessful despite Gayoom's ever-increasing unpopularity and his abuses of power which would culminate in his eventual electoral defeat.

Naseem moved quite decisively, given his resources and the capabilities available to him. In 1980, he joined with a group of Nasir loyalists to engage the services of nine former members of the British Special Air Service (SAS) to stage a coup to oust Gayoom. The fact that Naseem thought that a force of nine would suffice to oust Gayoom is instructive of his assessment of the country's limited military capabilities, which even in 1988 were extraordinarily poor. This coup attempt was shambolic, and although the arms needed – light weapons – arrived, smuggled in diving equipment, Gayoom's administration was alerted to their presence and moved decisively to end the insurgency before it even started. After the abject failure of this coup attempt, Naseem was duly tried and convicted for his involvement and was sentenced to life imprisonment.[22]

In 1983, a local shipping magnate, Reeko Ibrahim Maniku, sought to depose Gayoom through a much more subtle and more difficult to counter mechanism – a parliamentary coup. As the presidential nominee was decided by parliament, Maniku decided on what might be considered quite a potentially effective strategy – he sought to bribe the members ofpParliament as well as the High Court judges who might adjudicate on the candidacy for president. This parliamentary coup, like its more violent counterpart of 1980, failed spectacularly and Maniku was unable to stop Gayoom's nomination and victory, nor able to counter the inevitable rise of Gayoom's power.[23] To give credit, Maniku, though he remained in exile until 2006, did move to enter the democratic process by registering the Social Democratic Party in the years following his return.

These failures did not deter Gayoom's opponents, one of whom, Abdullah Luthufee, was to emerge and almost succeed in orchestrating a spectacularly effective coup with the support of a significant force of Sri Lankan mercenaries. Luthufee was a wealthy businessman with a near-pathological hatred for Gayoom. Gayoom's re-election as president with an even greater 'mandate' on 23 September 1988 (unsurprisingly, as he was again the only candidate) only served to antagonise Luthufee to an even greater extent, and he began plotting to overthrow Gayoom, this time with more money, firepower and trained personnel being committed to the effort.

Luthufee articulated his opposition to Gayoom and his regime in more democratic terms and had some legitimacy as a businessman. He established himself in the 1980s in Sri Lanka, where he operated a duck farm at Kadawatha. He was firmly of the view that the electoral process in the Maldives was fatally flawed and that the system would never allow any opposition party or candidate for the presidency a fair chance at winning any election in the country. Though it perhaps now seems counterintuitive, he was firmly convinced that an armed insurrection would have the open support of a substantial majority of the country, and that the state's sole security force – the National Security Service (NSS) – would at least tacitly support his effort as they too were increasingly discontented with Gayoom's regime. He was to be sadly mistaken in respect of the latter, and would pay a high price for it. However, his location in Sri Lanka enabled him to make and meet the acquaintance of well-armed and well-trained personnel of that country's Tamil insurgents, who were ideally placed to provide him with the services he required and were themselves eager for money to fund their own activities.[24]

The Sri Lanka Factor – Guns for Hire

Sri Lanka and the Maldives have a rather interesting relationship, though not one particularly relevant to the events of 1988. An ancient Maldivian legend tells a story about a twelfth century Sri Lankan prince named Koi Malé who was stranded in a Maldivian lagoon with his wife, who was the daughter of a Sinhalese king. Koi Malé would go on to establish a new kingdom and rule the country as its first sultan. True or not, it seemed in 1988 as if another Sri Lankan group was trying to replay this event, when Uma Maheswaran, leader of the militant Sri Lankan PLOTE group, on behalf of Luthufee, landed a force 80 well-armed mercenaries to establish a new system of rule in the islands. Sri Lanka's Tamil insurgents thus became guns for hire in this venture.

However, the Tamil fighters were no poorly trained rabble. They were generally highly motivated and well trained, and were given adequate weaponry, either through their own efforts – smuggling or manufacture of weapons including mortars and rocket launchers – or from India, which provided a degree of support and training to a large number of Tamil groups, out of which it hoped to exert a degree of influence on the course of the movement. Yet the Indians were not the driving force behind the Tamil insurgency, which instead had its roots in a rather unsavoury and tragic series of ultimately unforced errors that pitted ethnic Tamils against ethnic Sinhalese, with violence that killed thousands.

The roots of their motivation lay in the devastating Sri Lankan Civil War, which lasted until 2009 and perhaps had its beginning in 1971, though its most devastating phase lasted from about 1983–1987. Nearly 75 percent of Sri Lanka's population is comprised of predominantly Buddhist Sinhalese, while a little over 11 percent is ethnically Tamil. Some 70 percent of the population is Buddhist and over 12 percent is Hindu. However, unlike India – which, though it is 78–80 percent Hindu, is a secular state – Sri Lanka has Buddhism as its de facto state religion. Furthermore, the country's constitution explicitly states, at Chapter II Article 9, that foremost importance shall be given to Buddhism and that the state shall 'foster' that religion.

Following independence from the United Kingdom in 1948, the Sri Lankan Sinhalese majority, which now held the reins of power, began a series of measures that actively discriminated against the Sri Lankan Tamils. The first of these was the Ceylon Citizenship Act, which made it impossible for Indian Tamil workers, who had lived for decades on the island, to acquire citizenship (this was not rectified until 2003). The second measure was perhaps more discriminatory to local Tamils and took the form of the Sinhala Only Act of 1956, which was propagated by Prime Minister S.W.R.D. Bandaranaike. This was seen as a deliberate attempt to exclude the Tamil-speaking

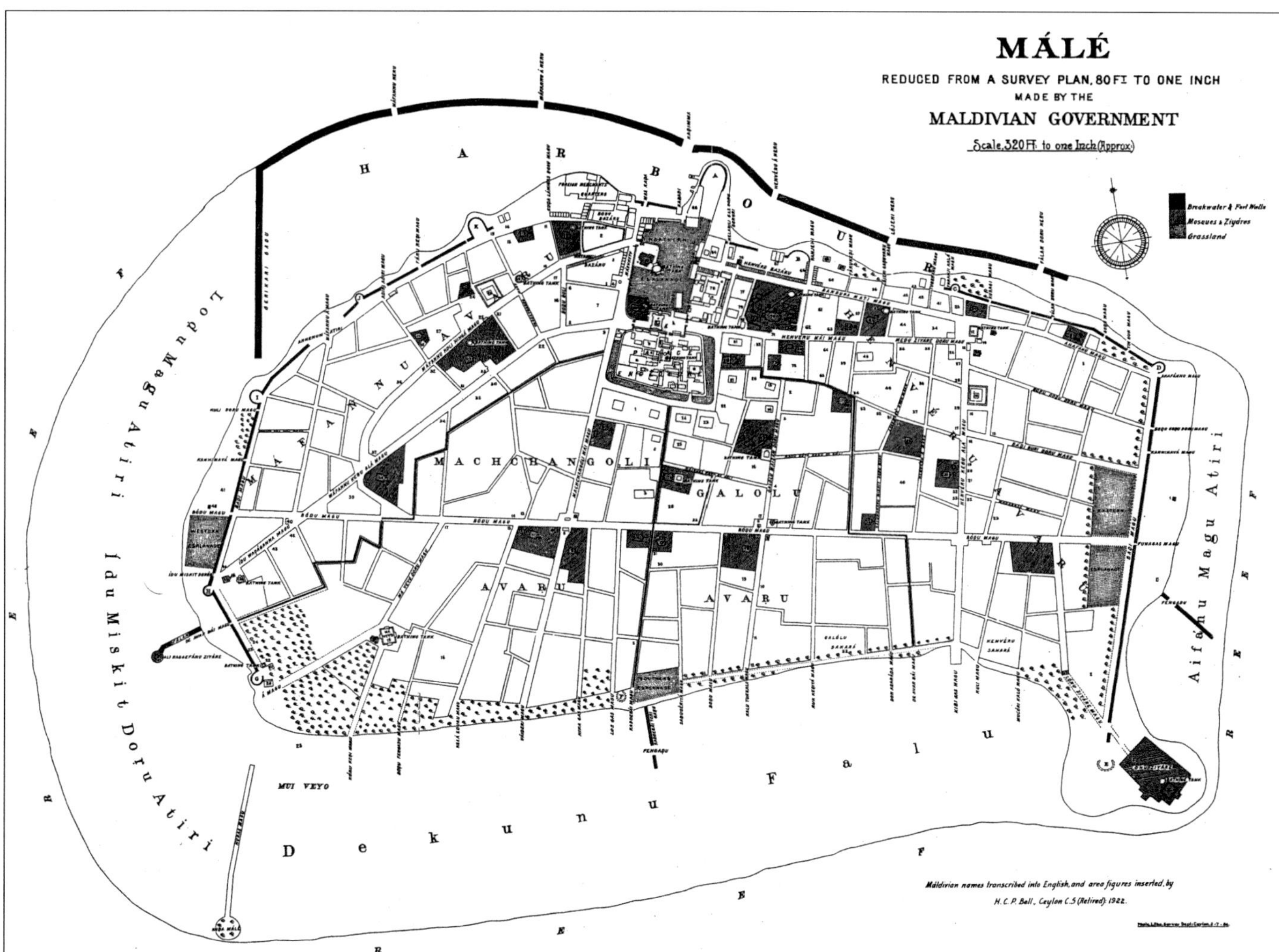

Map of Malé – capital of the Maldives – as of the early 1980s, based on a map from 1922. (Maldives Government)

minority from applying for government jobs, and the language requirement led to many Sri Lankan Tamils being forced out of government service.[25]

Badaranaike's assassination in 1959 resulted in a series of protests against the discriminatory laws, and this led, in 1961, to the arrest of several Tamil members of parliament and to a state of emergency which lasted two years. Rather than prompting a review of these laws, new discriminatory measures were taken in 1972, this time by Bandaranaike's widow, Srimavo, who had been elected to office and adopted a republican constitution. The new discrimination took the form of measures aimed at restricting the number of Tamils admitted to or able to access higher education. Tamil candidates were now required to score higher marks than Sinhalese candidates to access universities.[26]

These measures, combined with the democratic tyranny of demographics – the Sinhalese majority would always be able to dominate electoral politics and pass whatever laws they wished – prompted Tamil politicians to consider rather more drastic measures. This culminated in the Tamil Congress, the Federal party and diverse other groups coalescing into the Tamil United Liberation Front. Tired of trying to work within what they considered to be a broken system, these politicians took the drastic step of deciding that they would begin to campaign for a separate country – the Tamil Eelam – and that the achievement of this goal would, as party politics could not protect the interests of Tamils, be achieved by any means necessary, including armed action.[27]

This set the stage for the creation of an armed insurgency against the Sri Lankan state. The first such effort was rather surprisingly a left-wing, Maoist-inspired Sinhalese movement, the JVP, which launched its campaign to topple the government in 1971. The JVP attempted to reach out to the Tamil minority, but at all times remained Sinhalese dominated. Though it had a brief period of success, the JVP failed in its stated objectives of bringing down the government and was destroyed relatively easily. However, their campaign, which cost the Sri Lankan forces not inconsiderable losses, set the stage for the growth of Tamil insurgent groups. These were able to avoid scrutiny by the state and to build their resources while the Sri Lankan government was otherwise distracted by the JVP and its operations.[28] This failure to destroy these nascent groups would come back to haunt Sri Lanka.

The Sri Lankan Tamil insurgent groups went through a series of permutations, starting with the Pulip Padai (Army of Tigers) in the 1960s and the Tamil Liberation Organization of 1969. These would then morph and expand into a large number of groups aided by the London-based Eelam Revolutionary Organization, which established connections to various radical movements in Europe, including the Provisional Irish Republican Army (IRA), and also built links to the Palestine Liberation Organization (PLO). This enabled the training and equipping of the first serious cadre of Sri Lankan Tamil insurgents which would challenge Sri Lanka's government.[29]

Prior to the 1980s, Sri Lanka's Tamil groups, having seen the failure of the Tamil United Liberation Front (TULF) to politically hinder the discriminatory policies of the Sinhalese majority government which targeted the Tamil minority, formed small armed groups – among them the Liberation Tigers of Tamil Eelam (LTTE), the Tamil Eelam Liberation Organization (TELO) and the People's Liberation Organization of Tamil Eelam (PLOTE). These groups were mostly capable of conducting only small-scale operations such as bank robberies, a few ambushes and targeted assassinations of politicians and police officials. Their strength usually consisted of no more than a few dozen personnel armed with only small arms.[30]

However, in 1983, after the LTTE ambushed an army patrol, a wave of anti-Tamil pogroms swept Colombo, and this prompted India to start supporting several Sri Lankan Tamil groups.

The LTTE staged an ambush against a 15-man patrol of the Sri Lankan Army on 15 July 1983. This involved what would become an LTTE hallmark – the use of mines and IEDs (improvised explosive devices) to destroy vehicles. Despite being completely taken by surprise and at a disadvantage, the Sri Lankan troops fought back hard. Eventually, however, all but one of the patrol was killed. The ambush unleashed the events of what would be called Black July. In the wave of anti-Tamil violence that followed, no fewer than 600 – and possibly over 1,000 – Tamils were murdered, including 20 being burned alive in a bus. This tide of ethnic hatred and violence sowed the seeds for the Sri Lankan Civil War which compounded the national tragedy.[31]

The LTTE emerged as the strongest of these insurgent groups by 1986 – all but eliminating the TELO and forcing the PLOTE into a very minor position. This resulted in the PLOTE, unable to contest the might of the LTTE or operate against the Indian Peace Keeping Force (IPKF) operating against the LTTE, becoming available for hire. It was into this market that Luthufee's agenda and the needs of PLOTE became somewhat synchronised, though it is debatable how much the PLOTE cared for either Luthufee or the Maldives beyond their immediate need for money and possibly a new base of operations.

2 THE OPPOSING FORCES

The Indian and Maldives Military Forces in 1988

India's military in 1988 was in the throes of a transformation and was, albeit in a haphazard manner, reforming its security policy. Its principal foe, Pakistan, was rapidly modernising its own military too, and there was the spectre of conflict between the neighbouring states.

It would not surprise anyone to note that central to India's security is the fact that it is bordered by two countries with which it has serious border disputes. India has a volatile border with Pakistan, and in 1988 was having major issues with a Pakistani-sponsored insurgency in the Indian state of Punjab, along with the beginnings of a dangerous insurgency in the disputed Kashmir region. With China, the border dispute in 1988 was not nearly as serious, though there was and is mutual distrust between the two nations. This has meant that a substantial Indian troop presence has been maintained along the Sino-Indian border since the two countries fought a short but vicious war in 1962, and where there was a major confrontation between the two during 1986 and 1987.

India's internal security issues were substantial throughout the 1980s, with insurgencies springing up and intensifying throughout the country. From the north-east – with ongoing brutal ethnic violence taking place in Assam, Nagaland, Mizoram, Manipur and even Meghalaya and Tripura – to the Punjab, where the Indian Army felt compelled in 1984 to storm the holiest of Sikh shrines,[1] the Golden Temple in Amritsar, to neutralise terrorists holed up there, and to the increasingly intense protests in Kashmir – later to emerge as an armed insurgency – over rigged elections in 1987,[2] India's military was heavily committed to internal security operations. However, its forces were still quite able to also focus on conventional warfare against its hostile and very capable neighbours.

The prime minister of India from 1984–1989 was Rajiv Gandhi, the son of the previous prime minister, Indira Gandhi, who was herself the daughter of India's first prime minister, Jawaharlal Nehru. Indira Gandhi was assassinated in 1984 by her Sikh bodyguards in retaliation for the assault on the Golden Temple. This led to a vicious pogrom against Sikhs in Delhi, aided by the governing Indian National Congress. Rajiv Gandhi won the 1984 elections in a landslide victory and proceeded to begin a haphazard, though well-intentioned, series of economic and military reforms, along with an expansion of the armed forces.

In 1988, as now, India had arranged its conventional and non-conventional forces to deal with perceived threats from both Pakistan and China. In 1988, the bulk of India's troops were arrayed against Pakistan, but a large force of now fewer than 10 divisions – or close to 200,000 men – was earmarked for use against China, with some major forces being deployed in a tense confrontation with China in 1986 and 1987. The Sino-Pakistan strategic partnership created significant concern in India. In 1986 and 1987, China showed that it had few qualms about selling Pakistan missile technology, and in an egregious act of nuclear proliferation, supplied Pakistan with reliable designs for atomic weapons.

In 1988, India was plagued with issues of poverty, drought and an economy that was performing modestly. However, it was also at this point that a growing middle class was becoming increasingly assertive and important. This group, well-educated and articulate, began to see a role for India in the international arena beyond the very limited one that had hitherto been performed by the country and its military. This led not only to a re-evaluation of the country's foreign policy objectives, but also to an increase in its military forces and a revision of its strategic policy.

The post-1962 period saw a dramatic increase in size and capability of the Indian armed forces. Although the expansion was comprehensive, it was still essentially defensive and had little by way of a power projection capability, even to the islands of the Indian Ocean. The thrust of Indian defence policy was evolved around what the historian R.G.C. Thomas calls the 'minimalist' perspective of being able to fight one 'full' war and one 'half' war.[3] In military terms, this meant that India was capable of fighting a war on land, sea and in the air against Pakistan while being able to fight a defensive border war with China.

China was seen as the most significant threat to India throughout the 1960s and 1970s, and although the 1965 and 1971 wars with Pakistan proved that the Pakistani forces were a very capable adversary, the Indian leadership viewed China's military and economic growth in the 1980s with rising concern. It did not seek to match the Chinese effort though. Despite the substantial growth in India's naval capability and a widening gap in Indian air superiority, India had still confined itself to being able to fight a full-scale offensive war with Pakistan while deploying sufficient forces to fight only a defensive war against China.

By 1988, India had moved on from this position to one where it had the capacity to fight one full war and three half wars. This meant that India would be able to conduct a full war with Pakistan and a defensive border war with China, combined with a latent nuclear weapons capability and the ability to intervene in neighbouring Indian Ocean islands.[4] To this should be added India's nascent nuclear capability, which was being developed to meet a known Pakistani nuclear capability, while the first steps towards the development of SRBMs (Short-Range Ballistic Missiles) and IRBMs (Intermediate-Range Ballistic Missiles) were being taken to provide a baseline deterrent against China.

India's Military History Post-1971: A Synopsis

India and Pakistan fought three wars following independence in 1947 – in 1948, 1965 and 1971. While there was no major war between 1972 and 1999, the two countries did become involved in several military confrontations.

The first of these took place on 13 April 1984, when the Indian Army launched Operation Meghdoot to seize the Siachen Glacier.[5] Successfully concluded, this led to an ongoing confrontation between India and Pakistan where brigade-sized formations – with ample artillery support and sustained by helicopters – were deployed against each other along the 'Line of Control'. While the seizure of the Siachen Glacier represented a major setback for the Pakistani Army because Pakistan views the glacier as its territory, the scope of the conflict remained limited due to the area's high altitude and freezing temperatures.

The Siachen conflict blooded parts of the Indian and Pakistani armies like no other environment ever could, and turned many of their units into highly capable and experienced mountain and cold-weather troops. While neither side made use of offensive air power – the Indian Air Force (IAF) did consider the employment of its Hawker Hunter fighter jets – both made much use of heliborne logistics, with the Indians gradually fine-tuning their air support. While tensions have meanwhile lessened, both armies remain deployed in the field in this theatre of operations.

A potentially much more serious event took place between 1986 and 1987. In late 1986, India conducted a table-top exercise to explore new integrated mechanised warfare tactics. These evolved into a full-scale exercise – Operation Brasstacks – involving 150,000 men and thousands of tanks, armoured vehicles, artillery pieces and aircraft. However, a series of miscommunications over this exercise led to a massing of forces along the Pakistani border, with Islamabad worried that New Delhi actually planned a major strike to split the country in two with the help of rapidly advancing mechanised units. This apprehension did not result in a war, but Pakistan was rattled by the new Indian strategy and inexorably moved towards nuclearisation, followed by India.

India also faced tensions with China when, following a prolonged uneasy peace that began after India's defeat in the 1962 war, there was a sharp clash at Nathu La and Cho La in 1967 in which 88 Indians and over 300 Chinese soldiers were reported killed. In 1975, an incident led to the deaths of four Indian soldiers of the Assam Rifles in an ambush at Tulung La in Andhra Pradesh. After that, in mid-1987, Chinese and Indian forces were involved in a confrontation in the Sumdrong Chu Valley, prompting the then Chief of Army Staff, Krishnaswamy Sundarji, to receive permission to hold Operation Chequerboard, which involved a substantial increase of 50,000 troops to the strength then present in Arunachal Pradesh, while an exercise involving 10 divisions and several squadrons of the Indian Air Force was held. Three divisions at Wangdung were sustained solely by air, thereby demonstrating to China a capability to support forces in distant areas away from road links, which has proved to be very important for Indian units facing China ever since. The confrontation did not lead to any combat between the countries.[6]

It was into this somewhat usual security environment, fraught with tension on two borders, that then Prime Minister Rajiv Gandhi initiated Operation Pawan to attempt to force a settlement in the long-running Sri Lankan Civil War between ethnic Tamils and Sinhalese. The Indian Peace Keeping Force deployed, at its peak, some 100,000 personnel to the island and engaged in heavy combat against LTTE insurgents, with some 1,138 Indian soldiers being killed. In an operation lasting over two years, the IPKF proved to be militarily proficient but, as with all civil conflicts, unable to bring about any lasting peace settlement.

India's intervention in Sri Lanka, to which its involvement in the Maldives was but a corollary, was part of a broader redefining of India's view of itself and its place in the world. The country, which had hitherto been a poorly performing economy with endemic poverty and internal political turmoil, saw itself as overcoming some of the worst of its problems and emerging to take its place as both a regional and world power.

This was perhaps somewhat premature, and even today, although India's military capabilities, economic strength and development indices have improved by a large margin, the country remains somewhat cagey about deploying its military in support of its interest, except in humanitarian operations or under the auspices of the United Nations. Perhaps this is a legacy of the heavy casualties suffered in Sri Lanka in a failed effort to bring peace or a realisation that there are less-costly ways to achieve results using a combination of diplomatic and economic pressure, along with the threat of targeted military intervention.

The Indian Military of 1988

The Indian armed forces of 1988 were in the middle of a major expansion and re-equipment programme. This was largely done with inductions of Soviet bloc hardware, but also included a significant Western and locally made component – either by design or under license – in respect of both platforms and ordnance. Local designs of armour and combat aircraft had entered the design phase but were proving quite intractable and problematic, with major challenges being encountered with changing Army and Air Force requirements.

The Indian Air Force of 1988

Unlike the IAF of the present day, the Indian Air Force of 1988 had relatively limited long-range capability and was largely, in respect of its combat elements, a short-range, tactical air force. However, its transport assets were increasingly potent and were to prove to be an important element in India's intervention capability.

The IAF of 1988 was perhaps close to the peak of the service's combat squadron strength. Two squadrons of newly inducted Mirage 2000s – Nos. 1 and 7 – along with another two of MiG-29s – Nos. 28 and 47 – formed the cutting edge of the IAF's interception capability.[7] The Mirage 2000s, however, were still in the progress of receiving their complement of Super 530D missiles and Belouga submunition systems. The MiG-29s were initially armed with R-23 and R-60 air-to-air missiles, but the R-23s were in the process of being replaced by vastly superior R-27 systems in both their SARH and IR guided variants.

Augmenting the MiG-29 and Mirage 2000 were three squadrons of Jaguar fighter-bombers – Nos. 5, 14 and 27 squadrons. The former Canberra squadrons – No. 6 and No. 16 – were earmarked for re-equipment, and this was subsequently accomplished. The Jaguars were the most potent strike assets in the IAF at that time.[8]

Six squadrons flew the MiG-23. Four of these were tactical strike squadrons with MiG-23BNs, while two more were interceptor squadrons with MiG-23MFs. The latter type, with R-23 and R-60 missiles, was inducted as an interim response to the Pakistani Air Force deploying F-16s and were deemed to be useful but modest assets. The MiG-23BN was an effective tactical strike platform, replacing the Su-7 in that role.[9]

The MiG-27, which was now, alongside the Jaguar, being manufactured by Hindustan Aeronautics Limited, had begun to equip No. 9 and No. 222 squadrons and would eventually equip

A Mirage 2000H during pre-delivery testing in France. (Dassault, via Tom Cooper)

About 50 Mil Mi-8T helicopters acquired in the early 1980s formed the backbone of the IAF's helicopter fleet. (IAF)

An An-12B of the Indian Air Force, seen in the early 1980s. The type was showing its age at the time, and in the process of being replaced by a mix of turboprop-powered Antonov An-32s and jet-powered Ilyushin Il-76s. (Photo by Gulshan Luthra)

no fewer than six IAF squadrons. Among the items of ordnance obtained for the MiG-27 fleet were Kh-25, Kh-25MP, Kh-29L and Kh-23 missiles.

The MiG-21, in its FL, M, MF and bis versions (production of the latter only ceasing at HAL in 1987), equipped no fewer than 19 squadrons – Nos. 3, 4, 8, 15, 17, 21, 23, 24, 26, 29, 40, 32, 37, 40, 45, 51, 52, 101 and 108. While functioning as multi-role platforms with unguided rockets and bombs of up to 500kg – with the MF also capable of using the X-66 missile – the MiG-21 was primarily an interceptor and a mix of K-13, R-60 and R.550 air-to-air missiles were carried.

Alongside these supersonic combat assets were four squadrons of vintage platforms. A single squadron – No. 20 – continued to fly the Hawker Hunter (which also served as an advanced trainer) – while three more – Nos. 2, 22 and 28 – continued to fly the HAL Ajeet in the close support role. These aircraft were of limited capability but were all capable of carrying unguided rockets and bombs in the close support role. However, there was some work done in integrating the R-60 missile with the Hawker Hunter.[10]

Reconnaissance and electronic warfare assets rested on No. 35 Squadron, with MiG-21s and Canberras in service, No. 106 Squadron, using the Canberra PR.57, and No. 102 Squadron, using the MiG-25R. The latter two types were to provide invaluable strategic reconnaissance information over the course of several decades.

The IAF's combat assets included some 38 SAM squadrons – 30 using a mix of SA-2 and SA-3 systems and eight employing OSA-AKM (SA8b) systems. The IAF SAM inventory eventually replaced all SA-2 squadrons, which peaked at a strength of 21 squadrons, with SA-3s. The latter type, eventually equipping 30 squadrons, continues to form the backbone of the IAF SAM force to date, though it is increasingly viewed as being obsolete, despite upgrades aimed at keeping them viable against present threats.[11]

Combat assets also included four helicopter units – one (125HU) with Mi-25 gunships and three of Chetaks, one of which was equipped with SS.11B1 anti-tank missiles. The Mi-25s and SS.11-armed Chetaks saw extensive service in Sri Lanka, with the former

Prime Minister Narasimha Rao (centre, wearing white suit), with Wing Commander Ashok Goel, CO of No. 44 Squadron (right), in front of the first Il-76MD delivered to India in 1985. (Indian MOD Release)

even dropping 250kg bombs in addition to its more usual 57mm rockets and AT-2 'Swatter' anti-tank missiles (plus its 12.7mm rotary machine gun), while the Chetaks and their SS.11B1s were deployed for 'precision' strikes. Four additional units used the Cheetah for liaison and observation duties and for light transport. The Chetak and Cheetah, despite being poorly equipped for the reconnaissance role, have proved to be very reliable platforms and remain in service until this day. The IAF and Indian Army aviation corps armed several Chetaks and Cheetahs with 7.62mm MAG machine guns during Operation Pawan, and viewed this particular modification as being very effective and surprisingly versatile for supporting ground troops as well as deterring attacks on troop transport helicopters.[12]

Other helicopter assets for the transport role included one unit with Mi-26 heavy lift helicopters (126HU) and eight with a combination of Mi-8 and Mi-17 helicopters which could also be armed with 57mm rocket pods. The Mi-8 and Mi-17 units were to prove their worth during Operation Pawan and remained a useful asset for proximate interventions.[13] The Mi-8 and Mi-17 replaced the Mi-4 helicopter in IAF service and have proven to be the most effective medium-lift helicopters operated by the IAF since its inception.

In 1988, their potential was still being realised, with more and more Indian soldiers becoming used to heliborne operations and new tactics being devised to make effective use of these assets on the subcontinental battlefield. However, their numbers were as yet relatively modest and would require judicious use to achieve the greatest effect. This was not always easy as the IAF as yet lacked full night-operations capability for the type, and this led to complications.

The IAF also maintained a large transport fleet, largely of tactical transports but including some significant strategic transport assets. Rather surprisingly, two squadrons of vintage platforms still soldiered on. One squadron still flew the DHC-3 Otter, which used its STOL capabilities to great effect. Another squadron (No. 33) may have still operated a few DHC-4 Caribous, which though nominally withdrawn in 1986, might still have had a presence in IAF service.[14]

The HAL-built HS.748 filled a multiplicity of tasks, with some 60 aircraft being in IAF service. They aided in the carriage of freight, the transport of personnel and liaison tasks. Though not designed as a military transport, the type performed good service for the IAF and remains in service to date, despite its evident shortcomings.[15]

From 1984 onwards, the IAF began receiving An-32 tactical transports, and their induction into six squadrons was able to completely transform the air force's airlift capabilities with their enhanced payload and troop transport capabilities. They were used extensively to support Indian troops during Operation Pawan, and the six squadrons of the type continue to form the backbone of India's tactical transport fleet to this day. The An-32 was reportedly specially aimed at the Indian market as the An-26 was deemed by the IAF to have a wholly inadequate performance from 'hot and high' airfields.[16]

Strategic airlift in 1988 was provided by one squadron of An-12 (No. 25) and one of Il-76 (No. 44) heavy transports. Sufficient Il-76 aircraft would be obtained to allow the conversion of one flight of No. 25 Squadron (the other operating An-32s), but in 1988, the An-12 and Il-76 reigned as the IAF's long-range transport assets and were to prove decisive during Operation Cactus.[17] The An-12s were adapted for use as makeshift bombers during the 1971 war and were reputed to be very effective in that role.

It should also be noted that many Indian Air Force combat types – MiG-21s, MiG-27s and Jaguars – its training aircraft – the HPT-32, HT-2 and HJT-16 – as well the Chetak and Cheetah helicopters, alongside the HS-748 transport, were being manufactured either under license or as indigenous designs by Hindustan Aeronautics Limited (HAL). While there were undoubtedly problems with HAL's production, schedules and quality, its effort contributed enormously to the growth and modernisation of the IAF between the 1970s and 1980s.

The Indian Navy in 1988

The Indian Navy of 1988 was a large and growing force. At its core were two aircraft carriers – INS *Vikrant* and INS *Viraat* – each of which operated a mixed air group of British Aerospace Sea Harrier FRS.Mk 51 combat aircraft (30 of which were acquired by the Indian Navy) armed with Matra R.550 Magic Mk.I air-to-air missiles and Sea Eagle anti-ship missiles, Westland Sea King Mk.42A/B/C helicopters (some 40 being acquired, with the B version carrying Sea Eagle missiles in addition to the Anti Submarine Warfare gear of the A model) and Chetak helicopters in the search-and-rescue (SAR) role. Fourteen submarines – eight Foxtrot-class, four Kilo-class and two Type 1500-class – were in service, all armed with 533mm torpedoes.[18] A single Charlie-1-class cruise missile submarine (SSGN) – INS *Chakra* – was in service but was returned to the Soviet Union when its three-year lease expired in 1991.

These were escorted by five Rajput-class (modified Kashin-class) air defence destroyers (armed with Soviet-made SA-N-1 SAMs, SS-N-2C anti-ship missiles and Kamov Ka-25 helicopters) and three Godavari-class anti-submarine warfare frigates (fitted with Soviet-made SA-N-4 SAMs and SS-N-2C anti-ship missiles, along with two Sea King helicopters – one often replaced with a Chetak). The latter were heavily upgraded and modified versions of the Leander-class, six of which still served the Indian Navy as anti-submarine warfare escorts and, with their 4½-inch guns (also carrying British-made GWS.24 Seacat SAMs and a Chetak or Sea King helicopter), as naval gunfire support vessels. Two Whitby-class frigates – INS *Trishul* and INS *Talwar* – were modified with SS-N-2C missiles and AK-230 (CIWS) close-in weapons system, and remained in service.[19]

INS *Godavari*, the lead ship of this unique class, based on the design of the British-made Leander, but largely armed with Soviet-designed weapons. (Indian MOD Release)

While the Indian Navy was increasing its surface fleet, it should be noted that the Rajput-class destroyers were its most potent assets, and even then, these vessels were carrying a somewhat dated armament by 1988. A pattern of periodic upgrades and overhauls kept the vessels viable; the fact that four of five of the ships are still in service is a testament to the soundness of the design and to its adaptability. The ageing SA-N-1 SAMs are still operational, perhaps indicative of upgrades similar to those done on the Indian Air Force's SA-3 Pechora SAMs, while Brahmos missiles replaced the SS-N-2C.

The Godavari-class, however, was a much more interesting project, starting out as a proposal to equip the Leander-class frigates with the weapons system of India's Nanuchka-class corvettes. An earlier proposal to equip the old Crown Colony-class light cruiser INS *Mysore* with this armament was seriously considered by the Indian Navy, considering that the cruiser's hull was in excellent shape. However, the ageing machinery of the vessel and the extent of the modernisation required militated against taking such a step, and the ship was decommissioned in the mid-1980s after serving for its last years with distinction as a cadet training ship. The Navy's experience with modifying the two Whitby-class vessels, with their delays and problems, was also a major factor in deciding against upgrading the INS *Mysore*.

The Godavaris then became an entirely new design, albeit one based on the Leander-class vessels. Appreciating the very modest anti-aircraft and anti-ship armament of the Leander-class – even as modified in Indian service – the Godavaris received a new SAM system in the form of the SA-N-4 and anti-ship missiles in the form of SS-N-2Cs. Appreciating the need for a CIWS, the AK-230 of the Rajput-class was added and the 57mm AK-257 from the Nanuchka-class formed the main gun armament, primarily in the anti-aircraft role, though with some anti-surface capability, all systems being radar-directed for dramatically enhanced accuracy. The anti-submarine equipment was also enhanced with new, locally designed sonar and two 324mm torpedo tubes which initially used Italian Whitehead A-244S torpedoes but later an Indian derivative, the NST-58. The biggest change was the deployment of two Sea King Mk.42 helicopters in a hangar, though most peacetime deployments were with one Sea King and one Chetak, which proved itself over and over as a versatile utility helicopter, performing everything from search-and-rescue functions to armed escort with 7.62mm machine guns and even anti-submarine warfare roles carrying 324mm torpedoes, though without any sensors for that task.

Surface combatants were augmented by 12 Petya-class ASW corvettes, used as light frigates, three Durg-class corvettes (versions of the Nanuchka-class but with four SS-N-2C missiles instead of SS-N-9s) and eight OSA-II-class missile boats. Coastal patrol assets included a number of Sukanya-class OPVs (offshore patrol vessels) and Seaward Defence Boats, all with 40mm L/60 Bofors. The Indian Navy was in the process of ordering a new family of missile boats – based on the Soviet Tarantul-class and to be license-built in country – some Pauk-class ASW corvettes to augment the Petya-class fleet and a new generation of missile corvettes – the Khukri-class, which would serve as a replacement for the Petya-class but with an emphasis on anti-surface as opposed to anti-submarine warfare. Of note is the fact that nearly all India's new small naval craft and its frigates were being designed and built in India. However, nearly all anti-aircraft and anti-ship systems – from missiles to CIWS to guns – were being imported from the USSR, though anti-submarine armament and sensors as well as surveillance radars were increasingly based on improvements to and indigenous adaptations of license-manufactured foreign designs with considerable local input and indigenous design capability being manifest in sonar technology for surface ships.

The Indian Navy was not shy of deploying its missile vessels and corvettes on deep-water operations, supported by the Navy's small force of fleet tankers, a significant distance from the India coast. The Nanuchka-class, while heavily armed, were poor sea boats

The Indian Navy's first aircraft carrier, INS *Vikrant* (R11), was nearing the end of its service life in the late 1980s, but its air component – including Sea Harrier fighter-bombers and Sea King anti-submarine helicopters – was well trained and would, once again, prove its worth during the intervention in the Maldives. (Tom Cooper collection)

A Sea King Mk.42 helicopter during pre-delivery testing in Great Britain. The type entered Indian service with two units, of which INAS 336 served as a conversion outfit, while INAS 330 became the operational unit, which frequently provided detachments embarked on warships of the Navy. (Tom Cooper Collection)

and suffered heavily in rough weather. The Petya-class, although possessing one of the Indian Navy's heaviest ASW armament – a combination of RBU-2500 ASW mortars and 533mm heavy-weight torpedo tubes – was armed with 76mm guns for its sole anti-aircraft defence. These vessels also suffered heavily in bad weather, and maintenance problems were becoming a major concern for the Indian Navy. Indeed, this culminated in the loss of one frigate – INS *Andaman* – in 1990.

Added to these must be included the two Leopard-class frigates (INS *Beas* and INS *Betwa*) of the training squadron, with their 4½-inch guns and 40mm Bofors L/60s.[20] These two old frigates were supported by INS *Tir*, a purpose-built training vessel which was armed with 40mm Bofors weapons as its primary armament. As cadet training ships, these three vessels served the Indian Navy extremely well and were able to carry a large complement of personnel, all of whom could be armed for dealing with low-intensity threats. Rifles and machine guns were carried by these vessels in sufficient quantities to pose a substantial threat to any lightly armed assailant, a fact which would become very significant in the anti-piracy operations undertaken in the early twenty-first century.

Naval aviation, besides the carrier-based Sea Harriers, included a fleet of some 40 Sea Kings of varying types, five Kamov Ka-25s and a large number of Chetaks in the utility role, but with some carrying ASW torpedoes. Pride of place, however, went to the three land-based maritime reconnaissance/ASW squadrons. These included INAS 310 with the survivors of 14 Breguet Alize aircraft that were formerly embarked on INS *Vikrant* (shore-based following its fitment with a ski-jump ramp for the Sea Harriers), INAS 312 with the first of a total of eight TU-142M Bear-F long-range MR/ASW aircraft and INAS 315 with five Il-38 May MR/ASW aircraft. These assets were to play an important role during Operation Cactus.

The Indian Navy traditionally maintained relatively modest amphibious capabilities but had in 1971 carried out a single amphibious operation to capture Cox's Bazaar in Bangladesh. Romeo Force was an ad hoc entity and comprised a single Gorkha battalion along with elements of the Bihar Regiment and some artillery. These were embarked on a merchant ship, the *Vishwa Vijay*, and the troops conducted the operation against Cox's Bazaar between 13 and 15 December 1971, facing no resistance but also being extremely vulnerable to hostile fire had any been offered. It should be noted that the Navy's amphibious assets consisted mainly of landing craft rather than larger vessels.

By 1988, the Indian Navy had only marginally improved its amphibious assault capabilities. Its assets consisted of one vessel, INS *Magar* of a new class of locally built tank landing ships (the other, INS *Gharial*, would not be commissioned until 1992). Earlier, one ex-Royal Navy LST-3-class tank landing ship, rechristened INS *Magar* – which was purchased in 1951 and which was effectively awaiting disposal by 1988 – was the sole LST possessed by the Indian Navy. Other assets included some six out of an order of 10 Polnocny-class landing ships and six locally designed and built Vasco da Gama-class LCUs (Landing Craft Utility), each capable of carrying 120 troops and 250 tons of cargo. India possessed, in 1988, the ability to transport a small brigade with supporting equipment if all its amphibious assets could be brought to bear for the task.[21]

It should also be noted that, like the Indian Air Force, the Indian Navy was supported by a strong, if none-too-sophisticated, domestic industry. Indian shipyards built several patrol vessels, six Leander-class frigates, the three vessels of the Godavari-class and a number of amphibious warfare vessels. While there were significant issues with the cost, poor delivery schedules and even the quality of Indian-built ships, there was progressive improvement and local designs were encouraged, standing the Navy in good stead into the twenty-first century.

The Indian Army of 1988

In 1988, the Indian Army maintained Intervention Units at the battalion, brigade and divisional level. At battalion level were the para commando battalions; at brigade level the 340th Independent Brigade and the 50th Para Brigade; and at division level the 54th Air Assault Division.

The Indian Army of 1988 consisted of 10 corps-sized formations, with a total of 36 divisions and a number of independent brigades. The cutting edge of the Indian Army is centred around two powerful Strike Corps – each built around one armoured division. The other eight corps are defined as Holding Corps, though they may have significant offensive potential. The Indian Army was in the throes of a reorganisation programme in 1988, and this meant that several formations were being converted and re-tasked while being re-equipped.[22]

The basic infantry fighting formation in the Indian Army was and is the battalion, which is composed of four rifle companies and headquarters and support companies. Its heaviest weapons are generally mortars and machine guns, though some may also have anti-tank and surface-to-air missiles. In addition to basic infantry battalions, mechanised, parachute and commando battalions also exist, each created, trained and equipped for a special role.

Artillery and armoured formations have battalion-sized equivalents called regiments. These are organised in a similar manner – armoured regiments have four tank squadrons, while artillery regiments have either three or four artillery batteries. All of these formations are of similar size, about 1,000-men strong. Battalion-sized formations are amalgamated with other formations to form brigades.

In the Indian Army, the most important formation is the brigade. Like the battalion, there are armour and artillery equivalents, but all share a basic similarity of structure. A brigade consists of three battalions or regiments and is usually provided with some supporting equipment – artillery and heavy mortars in the case of armour and infantry units. Some brigades, however, are designed to operate independently, and these are given more supporting elements, including engineering and signals as well as additional artillery.

Brigades are usually grouped together, with additional artillery, engineering, signals and other support elements, to form a division. India and Pakistan operate two basic

Table 1: Indian Army Commands, 1988

Command	Headquarters	Subordinate Units (Base)
HQ Indian Army	New Delhi	50th Independent Parachute Brigade (Agra)
Central Command	Lucknow	I Corps (currently assigned to South Western Command) I Corps (Mathura) X Corps (Bhatinda)
Eastern Command	Kolkata	23rd Infantry Division (Ranchi)
		III Corps (Dimapur)
		IV Corps (Tezpur)
		XXXIII Corps (Siliguri)
Northern Command	Udhampur	XIV Corps (Leh)
		XV Corps (Srinagar)
		XVI Corps (Nagrota)
Southern Command	Pune	
		XII Corps (Jodhpur)
Western Command	Chandimandir	
		II Corps (Ambala)
		IX Corps (Yol)
		XI Corps (Jalandhar)

types of division: infantry and armoured. India's infantry divisions are divided into plains and mountains formations, which, as their names suggest, are trained and equipped to fight in different geographic environments. The mountain divisions are primarily earmarked for use against China, though they can be converted for use on the plains after re-equipment.[23]

A typical infantry division comprises three infantry brigades, an artillery brigade and an armoured regiment. Support elements include an engineer regiment (as described in Table 3), a signal regiment and an air observation post flight, in addition to medical, transport, supply and repair units. Mountain divisions lack the armoured regiment and tend to have smaller-calibre artillery. They also have more engineering and support/logistics elements than plains formations.

As noted above, the 340th Independent Infantry Brigade and the 54th Infantry Division serve as intervention forces alongside the 50th Parachute Brigade.

Infantry Weapons

In 1988, Indian infantry units were armed with the Ishapore 1A1 automatic rifle – a version of the 7.62mm FN-FAL – as its primary infantry weapon. Each section of 11 men was also issued with one or two 7.62mm 1Bs – local versions of the L4A4 light machine guns – and one 84mm Carl Gustav recoilless rocket launcher, though in 1988 Carl Gustavs were still allocated at platoon and company level.[24]

Platoon-level firepower was augmented by a 51mm mortar, and each battalion had eight 7.62mm FN MAG (known as the Ishapore 2A1) machine guns assigned to it along with six 81mm mortars. All weapons were made in India. In many ways, at section, platoon, company and battalion level, the Indian Army was almost completely supplied with local products. While there were issues with delivery schedules and often with the quality of weapons supplied, the Indian infantry was relatively well provided for with infantry equipment and was moving slowly towards an upgrade of their basic weapon.[25]

The Sterling submachine carbine – known locally as the 9mm 1A1 – was in widespread service as a personal defence weapon for section leaders and officers. A number of Kalashnikov variants were in the process of induction to augment the firepower of paratroopers and para commandos, but the SLR remained the main battle rifle.[26]

Interestingly, the Indian Army had considered procuring new 5.56mm rifles, and among those trialled was the H&K G41. A small number of these were issued to para commandos during operations in Sri Lanka. The Indian INSAS family of rifles and machine guns was at an advanced stage of development in 1988.

India's Parachute Brigade was equipped with standard infantry weapons, with the Ishapore 1A being the standard battle rifle for the para battalions. However, the D-5 parachute precluded drops with Ishapore SLRs, and many paras carried Sterling carbines instead.

Battalion support weapons were in the main unchanged, with the FN MAG machine gun and 81mm mortars dominating. The anti-tank weapons of the infantry battalion were in the process of changing to ATGMs (Anti-Tank Guided Missiles), with the Milan, Fagot and Konkurs entering service. Of interest is the fact that old SS.11B1s, widely used by the Indian Army in the 1970s, were still in service, being used in the bunker-busting role in the Siachen Glacier operation well into the 1990s.

Even in 1988, the 106mm M40A1 and 57mm M18 recoilless rifles (the latter being assigned to mountain formations) were in widespread service, with the former being a particularly useful weapon to 50th Para Brigade's battalions.

The 106mm M40A1, mounted on jeeps, was the principal anti-tank and direct-fire support weapon available to India's paratroopers. These weapons replaced 6-pdr anti-tank guns with India's Parachute Brigade from the mid-1960s and were, by 1988, becoming virtually obsolete in their assigned anti-armour role.

The issuing of ATGMs of the Milan type to the Para Brigade was in progress, and these would, as with the infantry, completely replace the old 106mm recoilless guns. The M18 57mm recoilless rifles took longer to be phased out as the need for their replacement was somewhat less acute owing to the threat perception posed by China.

Artillery

India's tube artillery regiments each possessed 18 guns, each divided into three six-gun batteries. These were classed as mountain, field, medium, heavy, para and light or heavy mortar units.

In 1988, the Indian artillery was in the throes of expansion and re-equipment. Traditionally, field regiments were equipped with the venerable 25-pdr of Second World War vintage, while medium regiments had the 5½-inch howitzer. India's sole heavy regiment had the 7.2-inch howitzer in its Mk.6 configuration. Other systems such as the Soviet 100mm M1944 anti-tank/field gun were phased out despite possessing a good performance.[27]

The 25-pdr was a remarkably long-lived weapon in Indian service which served with distinction from the Second World War, through the 1965 and 1971 India–Pakistan wars and well into the 1980s. They were only phased out in 1991, but continued in service with India's Border Security Force for several more years.

The 5½-inch gun and the 7.2-inch howitzer were also of Second World War vintage, and their replacements were in progress by either the 130mm M-46 or 155mm FH-77-B02 gun. The latter two types have emerged as the mainstay of India's artillery from the late 1980s to the present date.

The mountain regiments were – in the past – equipped with either 76mm Yugoslav-made M48 guns, 105mm OTO Melara M56 howitzers or an Indian-designed 75/24mm howitzer. The latter type proved to be a very versatile weapon, continuing in service as a lightweight, long-range weapon that even saw service in the 1999 Kargil War.[28]

India's first effort in indigenous design and manufacture of artillery was that of a modest replacement for the ageing 3.7-inch howitzers. The result was the sturdy, long-ranged 75/24mm pack-howitzer, loosely based on a Canadian design, which served with mountain artillery regiments for decades. This weapon, though firing a light 14lb shell, had a range of 12.8km and saw action in the 1971 India–Pakistan War in the eastern theatre. This weapon was successful enough to serve in the Kargil War of 1999, where it was used in both the indirect and direct fire role.

After the 1971 war, priority was accorded to replacing the 25-pdr in field regiments, and the result was the 105mm Indian Field Gun. The ARDE (Armament Research and Development Establishment) developed the 105mm Indian Field Gun (IFG) in the 1970s, which became a mainstay of the Indian field regiments. While heavy at 3,400kg, the gun had respectable range of 17.4km and proved to be reasonably successful in service. By 1988, the process of equipping all mountain and field regiments with the Indian-designed and manufactured 105mm IFG, or its lighter counterpart, the Indian Light Field Gun (LFG) was underway. These two weapons equipped a substantial proportion of the Indian field artillery regiments, with 25-pdrs and 122mm D30s completing the rest.

Medium regiments were in the process of receiving more 130mm M-46 field guns. This weapon was extraordinarily popular in Indian service, though deemed to be more suited to combat in the plains as opposed to the mountains.[29] The 122mm D30 howitzer was a less popular weapon in Indian service, and thus was largely relegated to the infantry formations deployed on the plains, where their traverse and decent range made them quite useful. That said, they were viewed as delivering too light a shell, and as such the type had few supporters.

A well-camouflaged battery of Indian LFGs during deployment in Punjab. (Indian Ministry of Defence)

The 155/39 Bofors FH77/B02 gun/howitzer was ordered in 1986 and was in the process of equipping 20 regiments. The Bofors gun was the subject of much controversy at the time of purchase, and plans to license-produce over 1,000 guns in India were scrapped, thereby totally disrupting the Indian Army's artillery modernisation plans for decades.[30]

Rocket regiments, of which the Indian Army operated five in 1988, were equipped with BM-21 multiple rocket launchers firing locally manufactured rockets. In 1988, 40 light regiments were each equipped with a dozen local versions of the Brandt AM-50 mortar, and these were assigned initially on the basis of one per division, with some additional units earmarked for the mountains. A single heavy mortar regiment equipped with 160mm Tampella mortars was also on strength, the last unit operating the type which had peaked at the modest strength of two regiments from 1962 to the 1980s.

Self-propelled artillery was very limited: 68 Abbot 105mm self-propelled guns and 48 Catapult 130mm self-propelled guns (the latter being a 130mm M-46 placed on a Vijayanta chassis) were the sole self-propelled artillery systems in Indian service.

India's 50th Para Brigade had maintained artillery units with 75mm pack howitzers, but these were later replaced with an Indian-designed 75/24mm howitzer, developed to replace the 76mm M48 Yugoslav mountain guns and OTO Melara M56 105mm pack howitzers. The field artillery regiments attached to 340th Independent Brigade and 54th Infantry/Air Assault Division were equipped with the Indian-designed and manufactured 105mm IFG or its lighter counterpart, the LFG.

Air Defence Artillery

The late 1970s and 1980s saw a plethora of modern air defence (AD) systems becoming part of the inventory. The pace of induction of the L/70 gun system was accelerated to replace the ageing L/60. A massive infusion of equipment from the former Soviet Union came to India's rescue. The L/70 gun system took care of the point defence, but the field army had been completely neglected. The ZU-23 twin guns and the Strela-2M (SA-7), and later on the Igla-1M (SA-16) shoulder-fired systems, were inducted for the infantry divisions. The armoured divisions received the Shilka four-barrelled all-weather mobile system for point defence. In addition, numbers of the OSA-AK mobile all-weather system to take on the increasing attack helicopter threat were also provided to infantry divisions. Meanwhile, Strela 10-M (SA-13) mobile infrared SAM systems were provided to independent armoured brigades and Kvadrat all-weather systems for area air defence of the Strike Corps.[31]

In 1988, the Indian Army Air Defence Artillery had, in pride of place, two AD missile groups – the 501st and 502nd – equipped with Kvadrat SA-6 surface-to-air missiles. In addition, there were 33 regiments with Bofors L-40/70 towed anti-aircraft guns and four with ZSU-23-4 self-propelled AA. These were complemented by a number of mobile point-defence missile regiments with OSA-AKM

A T-72M1, the principal main battle tank of the Indian Army since the 1980s, during an exercise in the Ramgarh Desert in north-east India. (Indian Ministry of Defence)

SA-8b and Strela-10M SA-13 missile units, with a large number of Strela-2M MANPADS being in service.[32]

Armour

Indian armour was and is divided into three basic formations:

- armoured divisions;
- independent armoured brigades; and
- armoured regiments assigned to infantry divisions.

Depending on their type, these formations were equipped with three types of main battle tanks: the Soviet-made T-72M1, modified T-55s of very diverse origins and the Indian-made (though British-designed) Vijayanta. The T-72M1 was destined to become the principal tank of the Indian Army, though in 1988 the Vijayanta held that position by quite a margin. Over 1,000 T-55 tanks were procured from the late 1960s, while more than 2,100 Vijayantas were produced in India between 1965 and 1986.[33]

The Vijayanta was issued to armoured regiments attached to infantry divisions, and while it had an excellent L7A2 105mm gun, its armour, 80mm thick at most, was deemed inadequate, as was its problematic L60 engine and transmission. The T-55, in contrast, had been up-gunned with the L7A2 105mm gun and was a well-regarded vehicle in Indian service, though its fire-control system was deemed inadequate.

India's Vijayanta combined the L7 gun with the engine, transmission and fire-control system of the Chieftain into a lighter tank with only 80mm of armour. Given the fact that the armour of the modern Centurion, which the Indian Army also possessed, was nearly double that, it is almost inexplicable why this decision was made. Furthermore, the engine and transmission of the Chieftain were not particularly reliable, so the Vijayanta was a maintenance nightmare.

Designed by Vickers for export and as a lighter alternative to the Centurion, the Vijayanta was the first modern tank manufactured in India. (Indian Ministry of Defence)

Vijayanta crews during a briefing in front of one of their tanks. (Photo by Kunal Biswas)

Nonetheless, the Vijayanta was built in quantity – augmented with direct purchases of close to 1,400 T-54/-55 tanks from the USSR and Czechoslovakia – many of which were to be fitted with the Vijayanta's gun. The Vijayanta became an Indian tank with high levels of indigenisation by content and value, and spawned many variants, including bridge-layers, recovery vehicles and the Catapult SP Gun.

The Indian Army had operated several PT-76 and AMX-13 light tanks, but these were phased out of service by 1988. An attempt to create a new light tank on the BMP-2 chassis was a stillborn effort, despite successfully being developed and demonstrated, owing to an apparent lack of interest from the Indian Army. This decision would later come back to haunt them.

The mechanisation of a number of infantry battalions was in progress, with the BMP-1 being used to equip some 25 battalions, augmenting older APCs (armoured personnel carriers) such as the BTR-60PB and the OT-62 and OT-64. The latter three APC types were by 1988 ageing, and the BMP would come to replace them completely. Some 110 BRDM armoured cars, along with two battalions of 'Striker' versions with Konkurs ATGMs, were also in service.

A column of up-gunned T-55 tanks of the Indian Army on a military parade. (Bharat-Rakshak)

The Army Aviation Corps

Formed in 1986, the Army Aviation Corps (AAC) absorbed most of the IAF's Chetak and Cheetah units into newly formed helicopter squadrons. The AAC operated over 100 helicopters of each type and was capable of conducting independent reconnaissance, liaison and surveillance operations without need for IAF assistance. However, in these tasks, the AAC was handicapped by the lack of specialised surveillance equipment on its helicopters, the absence of night-vision equipment and the very limited armament of its machines – limited at the time to a single 7.62mm FN MAG on a handful of aircraft for the close support role.

Like the Indian Navy and Air Force, the Indian Army was supported by domestic industry. By 1988, almost all infantry weapons were locally manufactured, while 105mm artillery and 120mm mortars were produced along with their associated ammunition. Production of the T-72 tank and the BMP-2 ICV (Infantry Combat Vehicle) was in progress at Avadi, and while the Indian Army used few local designs, production – with a reasonably large percentage of indigenous components – of most of its main weapon systems were in progress.

Indian Army Intervention Formations: The 54th Air Assault Division – A Premature Experiment

In 1985, the visionary Indian Chief of Army Staff, General Krishnaswamy Sundarji, began experimenting with converting the 54th Infantry Division to an Air Assault Division. The increasing strength of the Indian Air Force's inventory of Mi-8 helicopters, with their enhanced capabilities, lent itself to this experiment. Prior to this experiment, the Indian Army had conducted a single major heliborne operation in combat. This was the Meghna bridge heli-lift during the 1971 war, when a force of Mi-4 helicopters performed 110 sorties to lift the entire Indian Army 311th Brigade across the Meghna on 9 December 1971.

The 54th Infantry Division was raised in 1966 at Secunderabad, and its initial order of battle consisted of the usual three infantry brigades and one artillery brigade.[34] As part of the Indian Army's Strategic Reserve, consisting of some four divisions, to be deployed as needed, the 54th Infantry Division was used as an experiment in airmobile operations. In 1981/82, one of its brigades had been given training in amphibious operations, while in 1986/87, the 47th Infantry Brigade was given heliborne training as part of Operation Trident, which saw it flown from Hyderabad to Delhi. The unit was also involved in Exercise Brasstacks, which led in 1986/87 to a tense standoff between India and Pakistan, with the first signs of nuclear weaponisation of the Indian subcontinent emerging at the time.[35]

However, despite being renamed, albeit temporarily, the 54th Air Assault Division, the formation proved to be more adept at loading

Table 2: 54th Air Assault Division, Order of Battle during raising, 1985–1987

Element	Subordinate Units
47th Infantry Brigade	
	13th Battalion Jammu and Kashmir Rifles (13 JAKRIF)
	5th Battalion 3rd Gorkha Rifles (5/3 GR)
74th Infantry Brigade	
	4th Battalion Sikh Light Infantry (4 Sikh LI)
	5th Battalion Madras Regiment (5 Madras)
	22nd Battalion Maratha Light Infantry (22 MLI)
91st Infantry Brigade	
	4th Battalion Madras Regiment (4 Madras)
	3rd Battalion Maratha Light Infantry (3 MLI)
	2nd Battalion 5th Gorkha Rifles (Frontier Force; 2/5 GR)
54th Artillery Brigade	
	7th Field Regiment
	141st Field Regiment
	6th Medium Regiment
	278th Medium Regiment
	1889th Light Regiment

and unloading from IAF transport aircraft, as the IAF itself lacked adequate numbers of helicopters to allow for the full division to be deemed an Air Assault Division – about 200 helicopters needing to be allocated for such a task. With only eight helicopter units operating Mi-8s or Mi-17s, this was clearly beyond the IAF's capability, and thus only select company- or battalion-sized formations could be trained in effective heliborne operations.

Nonetheless, as part of Operation Pawan – India's intervention in Sri Lanka – the 54th Air Assault Division was fully deployed with an attached mechanised infantry battalion, a regiment of tanks and an air observation flight with Chetak helicopters. Its order of battle during this time – the formation was the first inducted and was not withdrawn until 20 March 1990 – was as shown in Table 2.[36]

Table 3: 54th Air Assault Division, Divisional Reserves	
10th Battalion Para Commando (10 Para Cdo)	
65th Armoured Regiment	
47th Infantry Brigade	
76th Infantry Brigade	
91st Infantry Brigade	
	5th Battalion Madras Regiment (5 Madras)
	8th Battalion Mahar Regiment (8 Mahar)
	1st Battalion Maratha Light Infantry (1 MLI)

Though it performed with distinction in Sri Lanka, it was rapidly recognised that the formation could not be deemed an Air Assault Division, and as such its title reverted to that of the 54th Infantry Division. However, its saga was to see an unusual twist in 2011, when the formation was converted into a Reorganised Amphibious Formation (RAMFOR), and it is now the Indian Army's division-sized amphibious formation, thereby augmenting the 340th Independent Brigade. It is an interesting curiosity that the 54th Infantry Division was one of the last of India's formations to use the BMP-1 ICV. As a RAMFOR, the division has a substantial mechanised component, with both tanks and BMPs being used by the formation during amphibious operations. As late as 2009, while much of the Army had replaced its BMP-1s with license-built BMP-2s, the 54th Infantry Division still used the BMP-1, though its obsolete AT-3 Sagger ATGMs were replaced by more modern systems.[37]

The 340th Independent Brigade

Until 2011, the Indian Army's sole amphibious formation was the 340th Independent Brigade. The brigade, styled as an Independent Brigade Group (IBG), was given its amphibious role in 1983 and traditionally conducts a series of annual amphibious exercises in the Andaman and Nicobar Islands.[38] The brigade has three battalions, usually drawn from the Indian Army's Southern Command, with an attached artillery regiment and armoured units as required. This unit was one of the first inducted into Sri Lanka and remained there for the duration of Operation Pawan.

50th Parachute Brigade (India)

India's Parachute Regiment was the repository of the Indian Army's elite troops. It presently has eight special forces, five airborne, two Territorial Army and one counterinsurgency (Rashtriya Rifles) battalions on its lists. Additional battalions might be raised in time, but right now, the regiment has chosen to maintain this strength.[39]

Plans emerged in the mid-1980s to take the three para commando battalions from the Parachute Regiment and bring them together under an individual specialised organisation, the Special Forces Regiment. However, these plans were abandoned, and they continue to be trained and recruited by the Parachute Regiment and thus must perforce remain part of the Parachute Regiment's order of battle.[40] The total strength of the regiment stood at some 4,500 personnel in the Paratroopers (Airborne), while the Para (SF) included about 1,200 operatives.[41]

Table 4: 50th Parachute Brigade

Components	Notes
2 airborne infantry battalions	
1 parachute field regiment (artillery)	9th and 17th Parachute Field Regiments in rotation
60th Parachute Field Hospital	
411 (Independent) Parachute Field Company	Bombay Sappers
622 Parachute Composite Company	
50th (Independent) Parachute Brigade	ordnance section
50th (Independent) Parachute Brigade Signals Company	
2 (Independent) Parachute Field Workshop Company	electrical and mechanical engineering section
252nd (Parachute) Air Defence Battery	
50th (Independence) Parachute Brigade Provost Section	military police
President's Bodyguard	pathfinder company

The five airborne infantry battalions of the Parachute Regiment rotate to form part of the 50th Para Brigade, alternately serving their field tenures in counterinsurgency operations or high-altitude areas. One of the eight special forces battalions serves in the brigade on rotation. One of the two field artillery regiments (9th Para Field Regiment and 17th Para Field Regiment) also forms part of the brigade, while the other serves out its field tenure on rotation. These artillery regiments are equipped with 105mm LFGs, while a number of BMP-2 ICVs are also available for paradropping operations as part of the regiment. The 252nd AD Battery uses Igla-1M man-portable SAMs. The Parachute Brigade and the Para Special Forces today make extensive use of the IMI Tavor, various Kalashnikov variants, PKM and Negev Machine guns, and have ample ATGM support with Milan, Konkurs and Spike missiles.[42]

It is interesting to note that the 50th Parachute Brigade is something of a hybrid. While Western parachute regiments – most notably the British Paras – are airborne light infantry, the Soviets (and now the Russians) evolved their airborne units as airborne mechanised infantry. The Indian paratroopers were initially organised as light infantry, but with the attachment of BMP-2 ICVs, standard 105mm LFGs and their associated equipment, one may legitimately ask whether some genuflection towards the greater firepower and staying power of mechanised units is being bestowed upon India's Parachute Brigade. The 50th Para Brigade is now a viable rapid-reaction unit with sufficient staying power for regional operations.[43]

The Paras

In 1988, however, this was somewhat less certain, as the Parachute Regiment was an amalgam of both special forces units and the parent regiment. The latter had its roots in the Second World War and has had many operations to its credit, including a battalion-level para drop during the 1971 war, and has operated extensively in military operations subsequently, primarily in the counter-terrorist role and as elite infantry.

In the 1948 and 1965 wars, India's paratroopers – for a brief period organised into two brigades, 50th Para Brigade and 51st Para Brigade – were largely used as elite infantry, 1st Para being instrumental in the capture of the Haji Pir Pass, and 2nd, 3rd and 6th Para being responsible for the capture of a series of bridges in the Lahore sector after heavy fighting.[44]

In 1971, however, while several battalions were involved in roles as both elite infantry and as special forces operators, 2nd Para was to make its mark by conducting a full battalion-sized paradrop at Tangail on 11 December to capture the Poongli bridge. This would cut off the Pakistan Army's 93rd Brigade from its lines of retreat to possibly regroup at Dhaka with the rest of the Pakistani defenders of that city. The operation, which remains the largest airborne operation undertaken in South Asia, included the drop not only of infantry, but also of artillery and support equipment.[45]

The Paras, following the 1962 war with China and the rush for re-equipment for an expanding army still then largely equipped with Second World War weapons and equipment, found itself being allocated a high priority – just second after the newly raised mountain divisions of the Indian Army – for new weapons and equipment. This saw the replacement of the .303 SMLE rifles and .303 Bren and Vickers machine guns with Ishapore 1A SLRs, L4A4 Brens and FN MAG medium machine guns. The 9mm Sten guns were replaced by new 9mm Sterling carbines, while the 2-inch mortar at platoon level was updated. The 3-inch mortars of the support platoon were replaced by 81mm mortars, while the 6-pdr anti-tank guns were discarded in favour of 106mm M40A1 recoilless rifles.

Led by Lieutenant Colonel K.S. Pannu, 2nd Para was augmented by the 49th Para Field Battery (with 75mm pack howitzers), a platoon of 411 Para Field Company for engineering support, a detachment

A rare photograph from the Tangail drop, showing paratroopers in the process of jumping out of two C-119 Packet transports of the IAF. (IAF)

The Indian Army's paras continued with intensive training al through the 1980s, especially once new aircraft types like the An-32 were introduced to service. This photograph shows a training jump out of one of the Antonovs. (IAF)

A training jump and landing of paratroopers of the 6th Para during an exercise. (IAF)

Troops of the 9th Para during an exercise, with the Swedish-made Carl Gustav rocket launcher. (Indian MOD Release)

Paratroopers in a Jonga general purpose/utility vehicle, manufactured in India on the design of the Nissan Patrol P60 4WD. (via Sanjay Badri-Maharaj)

of 50th Para Brigade's signals company, a surgical team from 60 Para Medical Company and a Ground Liaison Section, together with other support elements. The total strength dropped was 27 officers, 25 junior commissioned officers and 734 other ranks.[46] The Indian Air Force effort for this task involved a substantial proportion of that service's transport assets, with An-12s, Dakotas, C-119 Packets and Caribous being involved in providing transport for the assault force. This paradrop was largely successful, though widely dispersed and was partly effective in cutting off the retreat to the north of Pakistan's 93rd Brigade.

The Tangail drop was perhaps the Paras' finest hour, the only time the unit was deployed as a parachute-dropped formation. The force was dropped using 22 C-47/DC-3 Dakotas operating from Kalaikunda, with six An-12s, 20 C-119 Packets and two DHC-4 Caribous operating from Dum Dum airport. While it was intended to complete the drop in a single wave, with the aircraft being launched at 1423 hours, two C-119 Packets departed 20 minutes earlier with a couple of pathfinder teams, one being a reserve team. An elaborate deception operation, employing paradropped dummies, was also used, being deployed from two DHC-4 Caribous.[47]

While the drop was generally exceedingly smooth, one Dakota dropped its load of 19 troops from 49th Para field battery some 11 miles north of the drop zone. Fired upon during their descent, they had to fight their way out to join the battalion, not linking up until 24 hours later. One Packet dropped its load of a howitzer and two jeeps 4 miles south of the drop zone and, owing to Pakistani troops holding out at Tangail, this equipment could only be recovered a day later. Four jeeps landed in ponds that were some 5–7ft deep, and nearly half the battalion supply drop landed in water or in villages but was retrieved by first light on 12 December. Finally, one Packet with 40 troops aboard developed engine trouble en route and had to return to Dum Dum, with these personnel being dropped together with the resupply on 12 December.[48]

The Paras – 1988

In 1988, the Indian Parachute Regiment was at one and the same time both very similar to its current configuration while being very different. In 1988, the Paras were less concerned with special forces and were more of a traditional parachute brigade with airborne light infantry. In 1988, the unit had some seven Para battalions – the 1st, 2nd, 3rd, 4th, 5th, 6th and 7th – as airborne light infantry, a force of jeeps equipped with 106mm M40A1s, and two field regiments – the 9th and 17th Field Regiments – now equipped with Indian-designed 75/24mm pack howitzers. Otherwise, perhaps unsurprisingly, the Paras retained older model weapons. The main rifle was still the 7.62 SLR, while its support weapons were standard issue infantry weapons from the Indian Army's inventory, though experimentation with 5.56mm rifles was undertaken.

The standard parachute was in the main the Indian-manufactured PTR-M parachute, which was derived from the American T-10 parachute. The T-10 was delivered to India as part of the 1951 acquisition of the Fairchild C-119 Packet. The T-10 was used in conjunction with the reserve T-7 parachute. Also procured were the Adjustable Individual Weapon Case, the Container Aerial Delivery A-21 – which was useful for dropping from the doors of the Packet – and the Container Aerial Delivery A-7, which was used for dropping ammunition. For skid-board drops, the Container Corrugated Cardboard was procured. These American systems remained in service for years, and indigenous variants of them were produced for use by the Paras.[49]

The Paras were trained to drop using the PTR-M with their personal weapons – the 7.62mm Ishapore SLR being the main infantry weapon – secured with the Adjustable Individual Weapon Case and a haversack with ammunition and rations. Platoon- and company-level weapons, such as the Carl Gustav recoilless rifle and, to a lesser extent, the 51mm mortar, were also dropped this way. The Paratrooper's Airborne Equipment (PAE) bag carried such items as communication sets and batteries, thus enabling Paras to jump with reasonable equipment levels.[50]

However, while the PTR-M was simple to use, versatile and very reliable – with very few accidents being reported over the decades – and was compatible with use from aircraft as wide ranging as the Dakota, Packet, HS-748 Avro, Caribou and An-32, it was not technically compatible for use from either the An-12 or Il-76. For these aircraft, the much more finicky and troublesome Soviet-origin D-5 parachute was used. The D-5 was introduced with the Il-76 to India in 1984 and created some difficulties for the Paras in adjusting to this newer and arguably less versatile equipment for routine paradrop operations. The D-5 had one very serious limitation – it limited the personal weapons that could be carried in a drop. The jumper fell assisted by a pilot chute. To avoid fouling this pilot chute, nothing protruding above the shoulder or below the knee should be carried. This created serious issues in respect of the long Ishapore SLR, not to mention support weapons like the Carl Gustav. For a considerable period of time, jumps with the D-5 limited the Paras to drops with Sterling submachine carbines which, as pistol calibre, short-range weapons, placed them at a decided disadvantage against reasonably armed adversaries.[51]

The Para Commando Battalions

The Para Commando units were created by the Indian Army in 1966. During the Indo-Pakistani War of 1965, a small ad hoc force comprising volunteers from most infantry units operated along and behind enemy lines.[52] The performance of this force proved to the higher authorities that such units had much utility and consequently there was greater emphasis placed on the raising of unconventional forces.[53]

On 1 July 1967, the 10th Para Commando was raised by splitting the 9th Para Commando at Gwalior. The Para Commandos were first deployed in the Indo-Pakistani War of 1971, with 9th Para Commando capturing a 122mm howitzer battery at Mandhol in Poonch, Jammu and Kashmir. The 10th Para Commando conducted a series of deep penetration raids into Pakistan, with A Group targeting Umarkot and a bridge on the Thar Canal and C Group storming Chachro, Virawah and Nagar. These raids into Pakistan were all successful and were accomplished with few difficulties for the commandos.[54]

The 9th and 10th Para Commando took part in the 1984 Operation Blue Star and were also deployed in Sri Lanka in the 1980s during India's involvement in the civil war, as part of Operation Pawan. They also saw action in Operation Cactus in 1988 in the Maldives and in the 1999 Kargil War. Much focus has been placed on the Para Commandos (now Para SF) units, as these are much more flexible in counterinsurgency and counter-terrorist operations.[55]

In 1988, only the 9th and 10th Para Commando battalions were in operation. These units received some training in HALO (high-altitude, low-opening) operations, as did a select number of paratroopers.[56] However, while they were the first to be issued with night-vision and night-fighting gear, in 1988, this was in acutely short supply. Moreover, while some efforts were being made to equip them with Kalashnikov variants as well as with a limited quantity of Western-origin weapons of 7.62x39mm and 5.56x45mm respectively, the bulk of even these special forces were equipped with standard Indian infantry weapons and their standard rifle was the Ishapore SLR.

The Indian Navy Special Forces – the Indian Marine Special Forces

In 1988, the Indian Marine Special Forces (IMSF) – which would later become the Marine Commando Force and are now known as the MARCOS – were the special forces unit of the Indian Navy. They were specifically created for conducting special operations such as amphibious warfare, close-quarter combat, counter-terrorism, direct action, special reconnaissance, unconventional warfare, hostage rescue, personnel recovery, combat search and rescue, asymmetric warfare, foreign internal defence,

Indian paras in full gear as part of the 1972 Republic Day Parade. (Indian Ministry of Defence)

Troops of the 2nd Para with one of their 106mm M40A1 recoilless rifles mounted on a Jonga jeep. (Photo by Kunal Biswas)

counter-proliferation and amphibious reconnaissance, including hydrographic reconnaissance.[57]

The IMSF were (and the MARCOS are) specially organised, trained and equipped for the conduct of special operations in a maritime environment. The unit is capable of operating in three mediums, namely sea, air and land. The core tasks of the IMSF include:[58]

- Conducting clandestine attack against enemy ships, offshore installations and other vital assets behind enemy lines
- Supporting amphibious operations including pre-assault ops
- Conducting unconventional warfare
- Conducting surveillance and recce missions in support of military operations
- Conducting clandestine diving operations
- Conducting hostage rescue operations in a maritime environment

The IMSF has its origins as far back as 1955, when the Indian Navy established its own diving school at Cochin, after sending students to study in England earlier in the 1950s. By the 1960s, two detachments – one at Bombay for the Western Fleet and one at Vishakapatnam for the Eastern Fleet – were established to perform salvage, clearance and underwater demolition. In the latter task, these divers were widely employed during the 1971 war to train Mukti Bahini (Bangladeshi guerrilla resistance) sappers and led several sabotage operations against Pakistani forces.[59]

When the Indian Navy began establishing the IMSF in 1986, its provisional commander, Lieutenant Arvind Singh and another officer completed training with US Navy SEALS. During Operation Pawan, the IMSF was to prove itself to be highly effective and conducted a number of missions to destroy LTTE speedboats and jetties.[60]

The Indian Navy began embarking teams of IMSF personnel aboard some of its surface vessels to conduct boarding operations that might require skills beyond that of armed sailors. This was to prove invaluable during Operation Cactus.

IMSF weapons were largely standard Indian infantry weapons, with widespread use of the license-made Sterling submachine gun and increasing use of Kalashnikov variants. However, their standard rifle, for some time, was the Ishapore SLR. The unit also used commercial-pattern crossbows for silent killing, these in due course being augmented by silenced versions of the MP-5.[61]

India's Intervention Capability in the 1980s: Paratroopers, Commandos and Marine Commandos

India has, since its independence, thus maintained limited but not inconsiderable forces capable of interventions outside the Indian subcontinent. At the core of this capability was and is the Indian Army's 50th Parachute Brigade. This, coupled with enhancements in the 1980s to the Indian Air Force's transport fleet with newer, long-range transports, enabled the 50th Para Brigade to further its reach. The Indian Navy always retained a not insubstantial amphibious capability. This capability, through a mechanised infantry brigade (the 340th Independent Infantry Brigade), was available for use during Operation Cactus, but was not deployed.

The Indian Navy itself was emerging as a major blue-water force in Asia, operating two aircraft carriers with escorts. While lacking a dedicated force of marines, it began the creation of a naval special forces unit which would play an important role in Operation Cactus. Also of note were the Indian Navy's aviation assets in the form of shipborne helicopters and land-based maritime reconnaissance aircraft.

The IPKF

A word about the Indian Peace Keeping Force (IPKF) is in order while discussing India's intervention forces. The IPKF was India's largest out-of-country military deployment. It remains to this day a topic of some unease within India owing to the somewhat rushed and ill-conceived deployment of personnel, as well as the unrealistic assumptions upon which its intervention was based.

The IPKF was the Indian military contingent, as part of a broader political objective, and was tasked with performing a major peacekeeping operation in Sri Lanka between 1987 and 1990 in pursuit of a political settlement between the Sri Lankan government and Tamil political forces and insurgents. The IPKF was formed under the aegis of the 1987 Indo-Sri Lankan Accord that aimed to end the Sri Lankan Civil War between the government and heavily armed Sri Lankan Tamil insurgents, most notably the Liberation Tigers of Tamil Eelam (LTTE).[62]

The tasks were assigned as per the terms of the Indo-Sri Lankan Accord, which was very much the brainchild of then Indian Prime Minister Rajiv Gandhi. The impetus for the accord and the IPKF was the escalation of the ethnic conflict in Sri Lanka between the Sinhalese-dominated government and the Tamil minority, and a massive influx of Tamil refugees in India. Rajiv Gandhi took, in partnership with a much more reluctant Sri Lankan President J.R. Jayawardene, the step of pushing through the accord and establishing and deploying the IPKF.

The principal objective of the IPKF was to disarm all Tamil insurgent groups, including the LTTE and establish a Tamil police force. The disarming of the insurgent groups was to be followed by the formation of an Interim Administrative Council as expeditiously as possible.

As peacekeepers, the IPKF was not envisaged as being required to engage in combat, and deployment and troop preparation were thus less than ideal due to this degree of naivety on the part of the Indian military and political leadership.

However, within a few months of their arrival, the IPKF, after some limited levels of disarmament by the insurgents, became engaged in heavy combat with the LTTE while trying to enforce the terms of the accord. The LTTE tried to dominate the Interim Administrative Council and refused to disarm. The handing over of weapons was a precondition to the establishment of peace and the enforcement of a political settlement on the island and threatened to wreck the tentative peace accord.[63]

The belligerent attitude on the part of the LTTE led to the group launching a series of attacks on the IPKF and the latter deciding to disarm the LTTE by force. Over a two-year period, while deployed in northern Sri Lanka, the IPKF launched a series of combat operations aimed at destroying the LTTE-led insurgency and taking over its strongholds.

Although it established a level of military dominance in the region at considerable cost, the IPKF never succeeded in eliminating the LTTE. A change in government in India, pressure from Tamil political parties in India as well as an increasing feeling that the effort in Sri Lanka was not worth the cost led to a cooling of Indian enthusiasm for armed involvement in the conflict. This was further complicated by political machinations between a new Sri Lankan government and the LTTE.[64]

The IPKF began its withdrawal from Sri Lanka in 1989, having received new orders from the newly elected government of Prime

Table 5: IPKF order of battle, 1988

Branch & Unit	Elements & Notes
Indian Army	
54th Infantry Division	
	10th Battalion, Para Commandos
	65th Armoured Regiment
	6th Battalion, Brigade of the Guards
91st Infantry Brigade	5th Battalion, Madras Regiment
	8th Battalion, Mahar Regiment
	1st Battalion, Maratha Light Infantry
76th Infantry Brigade	12th Battalion, Garhwal Rifles
	2nd Battalion, Maratha Light Infantry
	25th Battalion, Rajput Regiment
47th Infantry Brigade	11th Battalion, Madras Regiment
	5th Battalion, Maratha Light Infantry
	14th Battalion, Sikh Light Infantry
36th Infantry Division	
115th Infantry Brigade	5th Battalion, 1st Gorkha Rifles
72nd Infantry Brigade	4th Battalion, 5th Gorkha Rifles (Frontier Force)
	13th Battalion, Sikh Light Infantry
41st Infantry Brigade	5th Battalion, Rajputana Rifles
57th Infantry Division	Elements
4th Mountain Division	Elements
Independent Units	340th Infantry Brigade (Amphibious)
	18th Infantry Brigade
	4th Battalion, Mahar Regiment
	12th Battalion, Grenadiers
	5th Battalion, Parachute Regiment
	15th Battalion, Mechanised Infantry Regiment
	25th Battalion, Mechanised Infantry Regiment
	17th Parachute Field Regiment
	831st Light Regiment
	8th Engineer Regiment
	110th Engineer Regiment
Indian Air Force	
No. 33 Squadron	An-32
No. 109 HU	Mi-8T
No. 119 HU	Mi-8T
No. 125 HU	Mi-25
No. 665 AOP Squadron	Chetak & Cheetah

Minister V.P. Singh, who along with Sri Lankan President Ranasinghe Premadasa revised the terms of the accord, paving the way for the withdrawal. The last IPKF contingents departed Sri Lanka in March 1990 after suffering 1,165 personnel killed in action and 3,009 others wounded – though some suggest as many as 4,500 were wounded. LTTE casualties, while not entirely clear, were also very high, with those killed in action perhaps matching Indian losses.

The IPKF, at its peak, had deployed some 100,000 personnel in four infantry divisions, special forces units, aviation and armour, plus elements of the Indian Air Force, Navy, Coast Guard and the Central Reserve Police Force. The order of battle of forces deployed in Sri Lanka was as listed in Table 5.

Additional support was provided by Indian Navy warships and patrol boats, which were rotated on a regular basis, and 321 Squadron of the Indian Navy with its Chetak helicopters and 310 Squadron of the Indian Navy with its Breguet Alizes, the latter proving particularly effective in destroying LTTE speedboats. The Indian Marine Commando Force was also deployed to considerable effect, especially when considering their very limited numbers at the time. The Indian Navy diverted many of its patrol assets to the Palk Straits to interdict LTTE supplies, with limited results.

The scale of the Indian deployment was aided by the close proximity of Sri Lanka to the Indian mainland, but it nonetheless required a huge logistical effort on the part of the Indian armed forces and even its merchant marine to keep the IPKF supplied with munitions and fuel. The cost to the Indian exchequer was very high and weighed heavily on the minds of India's government elites.

The Lack of a Rapid Reaction Force

As impressive as India's armed forces and their potential intervention capability was on paper, in practice, the armed forces suffered from some significant deficiencies in respect of their ability to respond quickly to situations. The Indian armed forces, then as now, are largely geared towards protecting Indian territory. This inevitably means that units are deployed initially as defensive units and able to be mobilised fully in time to meet any attack that might materialise. India's air force kept fighters on quick reaction alert, and in border areas there were always troops deployed near to or at defensive positions.

However, none of the three Indian armed forces maintained any sort of quick reaction force. Some quick reaction teams were created in insurgency-prone areas, aimed at providing a rapid response to a terrorist incident or to pursue insurgents. At the time, as noted earlier, insurgencies in Punjab, the north-eastern states and Kashmir were severe, and as such, even elite units like the Paras were assigned to protect certain vulnerable points against terrorist strikes. At the same time, India was engaged in Operation Pawan, and little thought had been given to having to deploy troops further afield from India.

There were significant shortcomings that rendered India's power projection capability very limited. The Indian Air Force had only a single squadron of Il-76 long-range transports, and although the An-12 and An-32 fleets were quite capable of long-distance operations, anything too far from the Indian mainland would prove challenging. As of 1988, the Indian Air Force also lacked any in-flight refuelling aircraft, and none of its combat assets, or transports, were equipped with refuelling probes to make use of friendly assets that might have assisted. In addition, the combat fleet was dependent on tactical aircraft with very little reach beyond India's proximity. The exceptions to these were the Jaguars and Mirage 2000s.

The Indian Navy was better placed, with blue-water assets and two operational aircraft carriers. However, even they were handicapped by the lack of an effective marine corps. The IMSF was never intended to serve as anything more than a commando unit, and the reliance on the Army to provide troops for amphibious landings was not always ideal. The Navy had a very limited force of amphibious assault vessels and few logistics assets for out-of-area deployments despite their otherwise significant combat potential and capability with modern vessels.

Rather surprisingly, even the Indian Army never thought in terms of a rapid reaction force for external interventions. Despite the conversion, albeit temporarily, of the 54th Infantry Division to an Air Assault Division, the intention was never to use the formation to do anything other than operate within the subcontinent in the event of conflict with either Pakistan or China. Even the 50th Para Brigade was not envisaged as constituting a rapid reaction force at the time, as no eventuality was foreseen where such a requirement was needed. While any unit was able to be mobilised in the event of war, peacetime deployment in support of Indian interests was not deemed to be a priority.

India's diplomatic and political structure was also not geared up to respond to such contingencies, and while the country did have a cadre of regional experts and very capable diplomatic personnel, the idea of coordinating or facilitating a long-range military response at short notice to a request for help had not entered their calculations. The Indian diplomatic service and the Cabinet led by Rajiv Gandhi had to quite literally make things up as the crisis of November 1988 unfolded, and it is to the credit of all concerned that they were able to achieve commendable results and stage a very successful operation.

The Maldives National Security Service

The Maldives, in 1988, had a single armed force – the National Security Service (NSS) – which functioned as both a police force and an army-type formation and had a strength of under 1,000 personnel at the time. Its origins date to the establishment of the Maldives Police Force in 1972, with a security force known as the National Guard being a part thereof. The National Guard was renamed the National Security Service in 1979 (the designation retained until 2006, when the Maldives National Defence Force was established, separately from the police, which thus emerged as a separate civil-oriented force). The NSS included a small air unit, which – while a reasonably capable force, proving able to help maintain order and protect national interests – had no combat capability as of 1988. A small Coast Guard formed in 1976 had some 250 personnel and was equipped with a target-towing launch left behind by the departing Royal Air Force detachment. The vessel served alongside a 45ft-long Fairey Marine customs launch, bought in 1975. Three ex-Soviet trawlers, each armed with two 25mm guns, were handed over after being seized for illegal fishing. A Cheriton design patrol boat was purchased in 1984 and a 21-metre-long Tracker-type vessel was acquired in 1987.[65]

The Opposition: Maheswaran and The People's Liberation Organisation of Tamil Eelam (PLOTE)

PLOTE was one of several organisations fighting at the time for some degree of independence for the Tamil population of Sri Lanka. Its founder, Uma Maheswaran, was a contemporary of the legendary head of the LTTE, Velupillai Prabhakaran, and received extensive training in Lebanon and Syria from the Popular Front for the Liberation of Palestine (PFLP).[66] A dispute between Prabhakaran and Maheswaran led to PLOTE being formed as a distinct force from the LTTE. It took little part in the LTTE's campaigns and emerged in the aftermath of the carnage of the Sri Lankan Civil War to be a small, pro-government party led by D. Siddarthan as part of the Tamil National Alliance.[67]

PLOTE's history is a chequered one, and one which is reflective of the changing tides of fortune in the Sri Lankan Tamil insurgent pantheon. The organisation, one of the larger units of Tamil insurgents and well-funded through a series of bank raids, had been weakened by 1983 after being hit with a series of operations by the security forces. However, it staged a major propaganda coup when, on 23 July 1983, it launched a raid to free Tamil prisoners held at the Battlicaloa prison. This gave the group a degree of credibility in the eyes of the Tamil population, one which they would exploit and then squander.[68]

Following the events of Black July, PLOTE, like all Tamil insurgent groups, experienced a flood of enthusiastic young recruits who were all highly motivated, with the spectre of ethnic violence looming large and providing a great incentive for Tamil youths to take up arms. The group drew heavily in respect of its training methods from its Palestinian connections with the PFLP, which provided training to a number of PLOTE cadres. The group also established, thanks to its substantial coffers, a radio station called the *Voice of Tamileelam*, which broadcast propaganda in both Tamil and Sinhalese. It was a Marxist-Maoist entity in ideology and purportedly sought to build a popular base.[69]

Despite having a strength, on paper at least, of between 5,000 and 8,000 members, PLOTE was not a particularly effective group, with the scale of its operations never matching its supposed strength. This led to the inevitable conclusion that the bulk of its members were either non-combatants, not actually armed or trained, or perhaps kept as a 'force in being'. Whatever the case, compared to even smaller groups, PLOTE was not as aggressive in its operations during its existence. This inevitably led to a degree of disenchantment among its members, with the usual issues of camp monotony coming to the fore on occasion.[70]

On 21 October 1984, PLOTE staged its most daring operation when it attacked the Killinochchi Court. As is the custom in some parts of South Asia, licensed firearms belonging to civilians were lodged there, as well as a cache of weapons for issue to security personnel, guards for court prisoners and police personnel assigned to the court. This raid yielded the not inconsiderable arsenal of 72 shotguns and .303 Lee Enfield rifles, which, while dated, were still useful for any insurgent group. Another raid, on 25 April 1985, struck a police station, killing one police officer and looting the stock of weapons there. PLOTE had thus expanded its repertoire from merely conducting bank heists and minor operations to being able to conduct significant raids against defended targets, albeit not against Sri Lankan Army bases. It was able to carry out ambushes and minor raids against targets in Mannar, Vasivilan, Mullaitivu and Point Pedro.[71]

Like many insurgent groups, PLOTE had established significant bases in the Indian state of Tamil Nadu, where the population, being ethnically Tamil themselves, was very sympathetic to the plight of Sri Lanka's Tamil population. It was in these camps that things began to go drastically wrong for PLOTE, pitting them against both the elected Indian Tamil leadership in Tamil Nadu and the Indian intelligence agency, RAW, which was supporting and training Tamil insurgents. Uma Maheswaran's arrogance and authoritarian nature were to prove fatal for the group and cost them dearly in respect of materiel as well as goodwill, both of which they desperately needed.[72]

Maheswaran fell out with the legendary Indian Tamil Nadu politician Marudur Gopalan Ramachandran (popularly known as MGR). He also alienated the Indian government and military by unaccountably choosing to criticise the Indian Army's role in the Bangladesh liberation war of 1971. Indian support was drastically curtailed and PLOTE subsequently had to turn to purchasing weapons on the black market. A deal with a Taiwanese agent for 1,400 rifles and 300 submachine guns led to the arms cache being seized by Indian customs, and attempts to secure weapons from Palestinian sources were undermined when the Palestinian agent absconded with the money paid for a large arms shipment, hurting PLOTE's finances severely.[73]

Maheswaran, to secure his leadership, turned to torturing his own supporters with a series of purges and executions, thereby decimating the morale and ranks of PLOTE. Mass defections began to cripple the outfit and by 1986, PLOTE was no longer a factor in the Sri Lankan insurgency.[74] Maheswaran was thus isolated, alienated, held in low regard as a leader and in desperate need of funding and support. Into this environment arose Abdullah Luthufee's scheme.

In 1988, a force of some 80 PLOTE insurgents, armed with assault rifles – all of the ubiquitous Kalashnikov types – some support weapons such as machine guns and RPGs, along with, apparently, heavy machine guns, grenades and mortars, was offered the sum of between US$1 million and US$10 million by Maldivian businessman Abdullah Luthufee, who nursed a deep resentment that was bordering on pathological against the Gayoom government in the Maldives.[75] Meeting PLOTE though his business interests in Sri Lanka – he owned a duck farm – he apparently struck a deal with Maheswaran to conduct this overthrow of the Gayoon administration, totally underestimating the response from the international community, especially India, to such an event.

While the specifics of the PLOTE–Luthufee arrangement will be detailed later, it should be noted that the businessman underwent training alongside the PLOTE strike force and was prepared to share in their risks. Yet the PLOTE mercenaries were part of a dying movement, and their motivation and experience had to be tempered by the recent spate of bad luck that had been endured by their movement and the erratic nature of their leader.

PLOTE, like many Sri Lankan Tamil insurgent groups, had a tendency to assume that Indian support was inevitable, and a degree of entitlement had set in. While it is certainly true that Indian support came with its own agenda and was very much a product of its own domestic politics, the concern that Indian Tamils had for their Sri Lankan counterparts was genuine and should not be underestimated. However, as is too often the case, insurgent groups acquired certain levels of delusion, and began assuming that their patrons had infinite levels of patience and would tolerate any sort of conduct. PLOTE learned that it was unwise to alienate Indian support and would fade into oblivion because of it, but not before one last hurrah, albeit in the Maldives and not Sri Lanka.

The PLOTE insurgents were, like most of Sri Lanka's Tamil insurgent groups, armed with a variety of weapons sourced from diverse places. India supplied a large number of assault rifles, machine guns, rocket-propelled grenade launchers and explosives. However, few of these were of Indian origin, with RAW and the Intelligence Bureau deciding to procure weapons on the open market and supply them to the insurgents. This had the result of arming the insurgent groups with an eclectic collection of weapons which, while dominated by Kalashnikov variants, RPD and PKM machine guns and RPG-7 rocket launchers, also included US-origin M16 rifles and even captured G3 rifles from India's 1971 victory over Pakistan. These weapons were augmented by captured Sri Lankan Army armament and that looted from the Sri Lankan police, although in the latter case, the older .303 rifles were mainly issued to second-line troops. The Tamil insurgents were known to be particularly proficient with explosives and were adept at improvising their own weapons, and the LTTE in particular produced some ingenious and very effective heavy mortars and rocket launchers, which they would use to devastating effect against the Sri Lankan security forces.

However, in 1988, as has been noted, PLOTE was a shadow of its once more potent self, abandoned by India's civil and military hierarchy and completely out of favour with RAW. Like other Tamil groups, they would evolve a smuggling network whereby arms were procured on the black market and smuggled into Sri Lanka. While the LTTE were the acknowledged masters of this art, the PLOTE insurgents were also able to establish an effective supply network, although following the loss of Indian support, they often found themselves being duped by more unscrupulous arms dealers.

3 THE ATTACK

Abdullah Luthufee's business interests in Sri Lanka – his duck farm – and his wealth made him an attractive source of potential funds for PLOTE after their relationship with India had been wrecked by Maheswaran's own arrogance. For Luthufee, PLOTE, which had held itself out as a veteran force – having fought the Sri Lankan Army, the IPKF and even the LTTE – could be seen as a group through which he could achieve his ambitions of toppling Gayoom and bringing the Maldives, directly or indirectly, under his control. Whether Luthufee had any clear indication as to what the political future of the Maldives would be remains very unclear, and some have considered that he was a pawn in a larger game.[1]

Luthufee's Gamble

For PLOTE, Luthufee was a most propitious gift. His pathological hatred of Gayoom made him oblivious to the consequences of striking a deal with a Tamil insurgent group with the ideology of Maheswaran's PLOTE, not to mention Maheswaran's own somewhat delusional ambitions. Maheswaran, sensing Luthufee's desperation, seems to have been eyeing, in addition to the money that was paid to the organisation – purportedly some US$10 million – the creation of base facilities and securing effective control of a few islands in the north of the Maldives' archipelago. This would free him from Indian control, establish his own financing through gunrunning, narcotics and gold smuggling, and keep him far from the reach of the Indian and Sri Lankan armed forces as he would have the patronage and protection of a sovereign government.[2]

Maheswaran had some degree of confidence in PLOTE's ability to succeed in overthrowing the Gayoom government. His forces, as noted, had some level of combat experience and his surviving cadres – those who stuck with PLOTE after his purges of the organisation

Uma Maheswaran, the founder of the People's Liberation Organisation of Tamil Eelam (PLOTE). (via Adrien Fontanellaz)

with its attendant torture, murder and mass defections – were loyal to him and his authority. This meant that he could be assured that his forces would conduct operations as he envisioned them and not become creative or be diverted by frolics of their own. For the Maldives, this meant that the NSS would be confronted by a capable force, one which should be able to best them in any serious combat engagement.

Adding to their confidence was the fact that Luthufee, through his own network of connections and tapping into the disaffection with Gayoom's de facto dictatorship, had been assured of and indeed relied upon, the support of a number of former Maldivian military personnel. Among these were the ex-major Abbas Ibrahim and the former corporals Abdulla Shahid, Ahmed Nasir and Umar Jamaal.[3] Given the small size of the NSS and its very limited military capability, plus its diversion for other tasks such as routine policing as well as firefighting, it was envisaged that the removal of Gayoom and the support of some former personnel would encourage the rank and file of the NSS to be either neutral towards or supportive of the coup. In reality, this was to prove sorely mistaken, the support that the former officers promised being largely ephemeral as the NSS was to prove quite tenacious in its resistance against PLOTE.

The Plan

Luthufee and Maheswaran formulated their plans around an attacking force of some 80 PLOTE fighters. These would be armed with the best equipment that PLOTE had, the attackers carrying into action Kalashnikov-type rifles, grenades, light mortars and machine guns – both light and general purpose. One could suggest that the attackers were in effect a rifle company in respect of numbers and firepower, and though they would be severely outnumbered by the NSS security personnel, they would have had the element of surprise plus the advantage of experience and training that should have given them at least an edge over their adversaries.

Luthufee and Maheswaran began their planning in 1987, just as the IPKF was deploying to Sri Lanka and just as the fortunes of PLOTE seemed to be in terminal decline, with the organisation facing the spectre of being an irrelevant appendage or a footnote to a struggle fronted by other organisations such as the LTTE and India's own Sri Lankan Tamil groups. Both individuals, wary of repeating past mistakes, learned lessons from the failed 1980 and 1983 coup attempts. They gambled on staging the attack when Gayoom would not be in the Maldives, thus making the seizure of power much easier. The opportunity for this came when it was disclosed that Gayoom would be visiting New Delhi to commemorate the anniversary of the death of the late Indian prime minister, Indira Gandhi – mother of the then incumbent, Rajiv Gandhi.[4]

From their base of operations in Sri Lanka, the mercenaries would need to travel by sea to the Maldives. This in turn would necessitate an effective and undetected seaborne assault, as the attacking force would be most vulnerable to interception while afloat and relatively defenceless against even the small force of modestly equipped patrol boats operated by the Maldives security agencies. It should be noted that Sri Lankan and Indian naval forces were not deemed to be a major factor in the planning of this aspect of the operation; both forces were, in respect to the Sri Lankan theatre of operations at any rate, focused on maintaining as effective a naval presence as possible between India and Sri Lanka so as to reduce weapons smuggling and the transport of personnel for the LTTE insurgents who were by that time engaged in serious combat with the soldiers of the IPKF.

Once Luthufee and Maheswaran decided upon a seaborne assault, the requisite force was assembled for training at a PLOTE base in Vavuniya in northern Sri Lankia. Luthufee, whatever his motivations or

A group of PLOTE militants undergoing training in Sri Lanka in the mid-1980s. Sagar Ahmed Nasir is marked with the number five. (via Adrien Fontanellaz)

It might appear unusual for a military operation to start with the landing of a vulnerable transport aircraft, but this is exactly what happened in the case of Operation Cactus. Although uncertain about the condition of the runway of Malé International Airport, Group Captain A.G. Bewoor landed his Il-76MD from No. 44 Squadron in pitch darkness around 2200 hours local time on 3 November 1988, effectively opening Operation Cactus. At the time, the IAF had only quite recently acquired 17 such aircraft from the USSR. Locally designated Gajraj, they were assigned to Nos. 25 and 44 Squadrons. All had their top fuselage surfaces painted in white, a thin blue cheat line, and wings, horizontal stabilisers and lower portions of the fuselage painted in grey. Note the application of the service title (Indian Air Force) on the forward fuselage: in Hindi on the port/left and in English on the right/starboard side. (Artwork by Tom Cooper)

As soon as Malé International Airport was secured, an entire fleet of additional Indian transports flew in reinforcements, heavy weapons, ammunition and supplies. Among them were An-12s from Nos. 25 and 44 Squadrons, all nearing the end of their service but still in great demand and kept operational with the help of No. 3 Base Repair Depot at Chandigarh. By this time, all were painted in grey overall, with the cockpit roof in white. As well as their registrations – applied above the fin flash – they wore large black codes (apparently A to Z) at the base of the fin. Service titles were rarely applied on the IAF's An-12s, but this one received them in English on either side of the forward fuselage. (Artwork by Tom Cooper)

The third transport type deployed by the IAF in support of Operation Cactus was the Antonov An-32, locally designated Sutlej. This type was still quite new in India, but Nos. 12, 33, 43 and 48 Squadrons were working up on it. All received the same livery as the Il-76s, but some of the aircraft lacked their service titles. As far as is known, as of 1988, most had not yet received a single-letter code (apparently A to Z) applied in black behind the cockpit. (Artwork by Tom Cooper)

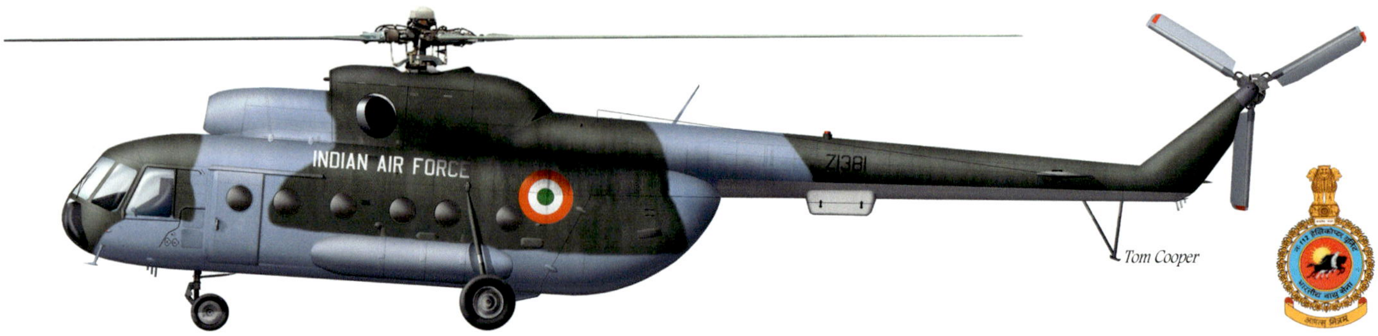

At the same time as the landing of the Il-76s loaded with paras, No. 112 Helicopter Unit of the Indian Air Force received orders to send two Mi-8 helicopters to the Maldives. Launching from Trivandrum at dawn on 4 November 1988, the two Mi-8s – piloted by Wing Commander S.K. Sharma and Flight Commander K.J. Bhat, and carrying that unit's technical officer, Flight Lieutenant Sinha – reached Malé following a hair-raising flight only metres above the wave-tops, despite bad weather. They thus became the only IAF helicopters involved in Operation Cactus. As of 1988, around 100 Mi-8s were in service with at least five helicopter units of the IAF: nearly all were painted as shown here (in blue-grey and dark green on top surfaces and sides) and wore four-digit serials prefixed by Z. (Artwork by Tom Cooper)

Aircraft and helicopters of the Indian Navy played a crucial role in establishing control over the sea between the southern shores of India, the Maldives and Sri Lanka. Foremost among these were Tupolev Tu-142MK-Es: the first three out of an eventual eight (all second-hand but overhauled examples) were delivered only in March 1988, and this was thus their first active operation. All the Tu-142MK-Es were operated by Indian Navy Squadron (INAS) 312, the crest of which is shown as an inset, originally based at the Naval Air Station at Dabolim. They were painted in mid-grey overall, but had the leading edges of their wings and horizontal fins, and the spinners, left in bare metal overall. National insignia was applied in six positions: on the rear fuselage this was followed by the service title (in English on the port side and Hindi on the starboard) and the individual serial number, the last two figures of which were repeated below the cockpit. (Artwork by Tom Cooper)

Another maritime patrol aircraft (and anti-submarine aircraft) of Soviet design in service with the Indian Navy as of 1988, and deployed operationally during Operation Cactus, was the Ilyushin Il-38. Three of these were acquired in 1977, with two much-upgraded Il-38SDs following in 1983. The Il-38SD included the installation of the new Sea Dragon avionic suite, new radar, forward-looking infrared turret under the nose, an electronic warfare system and compatibility with British-made Sea Eagle anti-ship missiles. Operated by the Dabolim-based INAS 315, all five were painted in mid-grey overall, wore national markings in six positions, with service titles and serials in black. (Artwork by Tom Cooper)

It is likely they were withdrawn in the 1970s.

The Ferrets augmented a force of machine gun armed trailer-trucks supplied by the United States but both the Ferrets and the machine gun trucks were supplemented and largely supplanted by a force of some 15 V-150 Cadillac Gage armoured personnel carriers.[19]

The latter vehicles were to become the mainstay of the Jamaica Regiment's protected mobility forces and saw extensive use during internal security operations from 1976 onwards. These vehicles were to prove particularly useful during the sporadic cycles of electoral violence to clear burning roadblocks as well as periods of urban unrest and violence, most recently in Tivoli Gardens in 2010.

Table 13: Legacy Aircraft used by the JDF Air Wing[24]

Aircraft Type	Quantity	Service Entry	Out of Service	Origin
Aerospatiale AS.355 Ecureuil	4	1999	2007	France
Beech A100 King Air	1	1975	2003	USA
Beech B60 Duke	1	1975	1981	USA
Bell 47G Sioux	2	1963	1971	USA
Bell 205A	4	1974	1975	USA
Bell 206 JetRanger	8	1971	current	USA
Bell 212 Twin Huey	3	1973	1998	USA
Bell 222UT	1	1986	1988	USA
Bell 407	4	2007	current	USA
Bell 412	3	1998	current	USA
Bell UH-1H Iroquois	4	1989	2002	USA
Britten-Norman BN-2A Islander	2	1974	2012	UK
Cessna 185 Skywagon	4	1963	1977	USA
Cessna 210 Centurion	3	1983	2011	USA
Cessna 337G (O-2A) Skymaster	1	1983	1994	USA
De Havilland Canada DHC-6 Twin Otter	1	1967	1978	Canada
Rockwell Commander 695A	1	2004	2006	ex-civil

The Jamaican Defence Force Air Wing

The Jamaican Defence Air Wing was formed in June 1963, initially as the Jamaican Air Squadron with pilots from the civilian Jamaican Flying Club. One month later the Jamaican Defence Force Air Wing was established on 3 July 1963 with the arrival of four Cessna 185s. These were later joined by a small force of two Bell 47G helicopters that were ferry-flown to Jamaica from Texas.[20]

Flying training was carried out in England until 1972 and after that in Canada, but Jamaica has made strenuous efforts to develop an indigenous training capability. From 1971 to 1973, the Air Wing received some Bell 206 and Bell 212 helicopters. The former type was to become a major element in the Air Wing's operational and training inventory, with a single type continuing in service to date. The Bell 212s, three of which were delivered in 1973, lasted in service until 1998 when they were withdrawn from use.[21]

In April 1977 the Air Wing became an autonomous unit within the JDF but was still largely subordinated to the Jamaica Regiment. A number of light transport and liaison aircraft were procured from the 1970s onwards with the Britten-Norman BN-2 being the most effective of these assets. However, various Cessna light aircraft were to predominate in the Air Wing, these being principally tasked with light transport duties with some limited use in the maritime

Bell 407 and Bell 412 of the JDF Air Wing. (JDF)

A Diamond DA42 trainer of the JDF Air Wing. (JDF)

Bell 407s and Bell 429s of the JDF Air Wing. (JDF)

patrol role, though they were never equipped with any sensors fit for the task.[22]

A modernisation of the helicopter fleet took place during 1989 when four Bell UH-1Hs were leased from the US government. One of these crashed in 1997 with the other three being withdrawn from use and returned in 2002. In fact, most of the Air Wing's equipment was sold in the late 1980s and 1990s. A fresh start was made at the beginning of 2000 when the Air Wing was re-equipped with the Bell 412 and Aerospatiale AS.355 Ecureuil. The latter type lasted for only seven years in JDF service.[23]

Like the Jamaican Coast Guard, the JDF Air Wing was to receive a new lease of life in the mid-2000s and has received a good deal of new equipment in the form of new models of Bell helicopters, establishing a very strong relationship with the Bell company. However, its fixed wing assets have not received similar attention and have atrophied.

The Jamaica Coast Guard

The naval arm of the JDF was formed in 1963, one year after the formation of the JDF. This naval arm was called the 'Jamaica Sea Squadron' and was established with an initial complement of three 63ft wooden Second World War torpedo recovery boats provided by the United States government. These vessels were commissioned (Her Majesty's Jamaican Ship) HMJS *Yoruba* (P1), HMJS *Coromante* (P2) and HMJS *Mandingo* (P3). As was common with the English-speaking Caribbean, a training team from the Royal Navy assisted with the Sea Squadron's early development.[25]

Some four years later, the Sea Squadron was renamed the Jamaica Defence Force Coast Guard (JDF CG) in 1966. In the tradition of British inspired forces, a naval White Ensign, naval rank insignia and Royal Navy-pattern uniforms were adopted. It should be noted that the JDF Coast Guard nominally holds army ranks – similar to the Air Wing and the Jamaica Regiment. This reflects the relatively subordinate role of the Coast Guard to the Jamaica Regiment and its land forces. This would seem to be counter intuitive for an island nation, but Jamaica's terrestrial internal security challenges have meant a focus on land forces.

In 1966, the JDF Coast Guard got rid of its wholly inadequate 63-foot boats and acquired the first of three 85ft all aluminium Bay-class patrol boats. These vessels, HMJS *Discovery Bay* (P4), HMJS *Holland Bay* (P5) and HMJS *Manatee Bay* (P6), were commissioned between 1966 and 1967. The Bay-class vessels were modified

Two Damen SPa 4207s of the Jamaica Coast Guard, in the company of a Bell 412 of the JDF Air Wing. (JDF)

Two interceptors and two Damen SPa 4207s of the JDF Coast Guard. (JDF)

HMJS *Cornwall* and HMJS *Middlesex* – both of the SPa 4207 class – seen while returning to base. (JDF)

commercial cabin cruiser designs and lasted in service well into the 1990s, though were of dubious serviceability. *Holland Bay* (P5) lasted until 2003, with at least two refits being undertaken.[26]

In 1974, the JDF Coast Guard acquired the first of two 'offshore' patrol vessels with HMJS *Fort Charles* (P7) being acquired. This vessel with a crew of 20 was 103ft long, displaced 103 tonnes and was armed with a 20mm gun and two .50 calibre M2HB guns. The *Fort Charles* was followed in 1985 by HMJS *Paul Bogle* (P8) which was similarly equipped.[27]

The ageing vessels of the Jamaican Coast Guard were augmented by two Point-class cutters, transferred in 1999 from the US Coast Guard – as part of a package given to several Caribbean countries – but these vessels do not appear to have served a very long time in Jamaican service. The smaller vessels of the JDF Coast Guard – Dauntless coastal patrol vessels and various interceptors – underwent several refits during the 1990s and early years of the twenty-first century.

Jamaica's principal patrol assets – the *Fort Charles* and the *Paul Bogle* – served for a long time but were increasingly obsolescent and refits produced diminishing returns. This led to their replacement in 2005–2006 by a fleet of modern Damen SPa4027 vessels. Nonetheless, the two ships remained in commission for decades though were of dubious serviceability.

Politics and Controversy – 1972 to 1980

In the 1970s and into the early 1980s Jamaica was plagued by intense political polarisation, some of it along ideological lines. Pro-Western elements were pitted against so-called pro-communist elements and with the ever-present threat of Cuban influence, a degree of political paranoia was present in the left-wing government of Prime Minister Michael Manley. These tensions manifested themselves in a series of coup plots, of varying levels of intensity. Manley's left-of-centre politics was inherently antagonistic to the pro-Western training and orientation of the Jamaican security establishment and political tensions between political parties and both the JDF and JCF were evident into the early 1980s.

Manley, in particular, reduced the level of military cooperation with the United States to minimal levels between 1972 and 1980 in accordance with the ideology of his People's National Party (PNP). The United States made no secret of its preference for the right-of-centre views of the Jamaica Labour Party (JLP) of Edward Seaga.

As far as the JDF was concerned, two alleged coup attempts were attributed to some of its personnel. The first was in 1976 when a JLP Senator, Pearnel Charles, and a former JDF officer, Peter Whittingham, were arrested for allegedly plotting a coup. However, evidence was minimal and the two were released.

Rather more serious was the arrest of 33 JDF officers and members of a right-wing party – the Jamaica United Front Party – on 22 June 1980. They were charged with plotting to commandeer two armoured cars and overthrow the Manley government after kidnapping him and killing the JDF Chief of Staff.[28]

These tensions and coup plots came to an end in 1980 when Manley was defeated by Edward Seaga in the 30 October 1980 elections and have not resurfaced despite Manley returning to power in 1989, chastened and somewhat more moderate in his views.

Urgent Fury – the JDF and the Caribbean Peacekeeping Force

The JDF had an important role to play during the 1983 US intervention in Grenada. Unlike Barbados, however, the JDF had little role in the planning or reconnaissance undertaken prior to the operation, and while Jamaica was supportive of the intervention, its government was not as proactive as the Eastern Caribbean States or Barbados in terms of organising or encouraging intervention in Grenada. However, once it was decided that a Caribbean Peacekeeping Force was to be sent to Grenada, the Jamaica Regiment was called upon to provide leadership and troops.

While Brigadier (promoted from Colonel for the role) Rudyard Lewis of Barbados was given the task as regional coordinator, Colonel Ken Barnes of the Jamaica Defence Force was given command of the Caribbean Peacekeeping Force. To the reinforced rifle platoon of the Barbados Defence Force, the one hundred policemen of the Barbados Police Force, and 50 assorted police personnel from other Caribbean islands, the Jamaica Regiment despatched a full rifle company of 120 personnel, a mortar section with two 81mm mortars and a medical section, giving a total of 150 JDF personnel being committed to Grenada, making it the only fully contained combat element of the CPKF.[29]

While the CPKF saw no combat, it was tasked with guarding prisoners, particularly those of the Grenadian People's Revolutionary Army, and with other military police functions. The Jamaica Defence Force personnel were much appreciated by their United States military counterparts and the strong sense of military professionalism enabled the JDF contingent to perform well and extricate itself from Grenada with no blemishes upon its reputation despite the fraught internal situation following the American military intervention.[30] No major allegations of abuse were levelled at the JDF units.

As noted in the introductory chapter, the Jamaica Defence Force has a good relationship with the Regional Security System and has operated in coordination with the latter on many regional operations, usually in support of humanitarian assistance and disaster relief. In addition, and again as detailed in the introductory chapter, the JDF was prepared to commit a full rifle company to Trinidad in 1990.

However, these experiences, and JCF support operations during periods of unrest, did not prepare the JDF for its most intense operation to date – in 2010, against Jamaica's criminal gangs.

The Tivoli Incursion 2010

The Tivoli Incursion was an operation launched by the JCF and the JDF to secure the notorious drug lord Christopher 'Dudus' Coke who led the infamous Shower Posse drug cartel in Kingston. The operation lasted a full month – from 23 May 2010 to 23 June 2010 – and saw the JCF and the JDF engaged in urban combat with armed criminal gang members. The situation was complicated by an apparent link between the then Jamaican Prime Minister, Bruce Golding, and Christopher Coke. The vast majority of the fighting in Tivoli Gardens took place between 24 May 2010 and 25 May 2010, though sporadic actions took place thereafter as the JCF and the JDF sought to find Coke and detain him pending extradition.

This was further complicated by the decision by the United States government to request the extradition of Coke in 2009, thus setting in motion a sequence of events that would culminate in the efforts of the JDF and the JCF to secure Coke and to extradite him to the United States. The confrontation that followed would cost at least 73 civilian lives, with four members of the security forces also being killed in action, several vehicles being destroyed and over 500 people arrested. It also involved the use of mortars on urban areas by the JDF as well as the extensive use of armoured vehicles by both the JDF and the JCF, with one of the JCF's armoured rescue vehicles being seriously damaged during the fighting, having been briefly abandoned.

The early sequence of events, in respect to the request for extradition and the process of proceeding in that regard, was described as follows by the West Kingston Commission of Inquiry, noting the roles of the Commissioner of Police, the Chief of Defence Staff (CDS), the Prime Minister and the Attorney-General:

> 3.5. On 24 August 2009, then CoP Hardley Lewin telephoned CDS Stewart Saunders and told him that a request for the extradition of Coke was to be made by the USG to the GoJ.
>
> 3.6. CDS Saunders and CoP Lewin went to advise the Minister of National Security, Mr Dwight Nelson. Mr Nelson was briefed as to the information, which the Heads of the security forces had, and he advised them to report to Prime Minister Golding. Accordingly, they briefed the Prime Minister at his official residence the same afternoon. Mr Golding testified about the information he received. Under cross-examination by Mr Linton Gordon on 11 February 2015, he said –
>
> "I did not get the impression from Gen. Saunders or CoP Lewin that they were seeking a direction from me. The USG wanted to alert me and CoP Lewin told them that it was his responsibility to alert me… I was alerted by the Heads of the security forces that an extradition warrant for Christopher Coke would be arriving the following day… I spoke to the Attorney-General late that evening to tell her what the Heads had told me. Ultimately, it was her call to make."
>
> …
>
> 3.10. When the former Attorney-General, Ms. Dorothy Lightbourne, gave evidence, she said that Prime Minister Golding telephoned her on 24 August 2009 and told her that a request for Coke's extradition was on its way. The next day, she received a telephone call from the Office of the Director of Public Prosecutions (DPP). It was the Deputy DPP who said that there was someone from the military in her office and the

person wanted to discuss the extradition with Ms. Lightbourne. Ms. Lightbourne said "I would not entertain it since it had not come through the proper channels, that is to say, the procedure and protocol for dealing with an extradition request had not been followed".

3.11. The proper procedure as represented to us was, in summary –

(a) A request for extradition is made by the Requesting State to the Ministry of Foreign Affairs of GoJ;

(b) The Ministry of Foreign Affairs then sends the documentation to the Ministry of Justice. An administrative officer prepares a letter in standard form addressed to the DPP and sends the letter and the documents received from the Requesting State to the DPP;

(c) The DPP prepares a draft of the document known as an "Authority to Proceed" and forwards it to the Attorney-General, assuming that the GoJ is going to proceed with the extradition.

3.12. On the morning of 26 August 2009, Ms. Lightbourne received a Diplomatic Note containing the Request for Extradition and the several supporting documents duly authenticated. On the same day, an approved document "Authority to Proceed" was sent to her.[31]

This process, starting in 2009, left ample room for Coke to be alerted to the possibility of his extradition and given his evident political connections, the Commission of Inquiry believes that it is probable that Coke was aware of these developments.

The JDF Chief of Defence Staff – General Stewart Saunders – and the Commissioner of Police, Owen Ellington – drew up plans and a joint headquarters was established. However, as the Commission of Inquiry established, the two did not plan in concert, with the JDF making its own plans and conducting specialised training:

3.25. Although it was understood by the leadership of the security forces that the operation would be a joint enterprise between the JDF and JCF, each Force developed its own plan. The JDF developed "Operation Garden Parish". The plan of the JCF was "Operation Keywest" which was the subject of an Operational Order. Nevertheless, a joint planning team met regularly. DCP Hinds stated that the plan to arrest Coke was completed in January 2010. CDS Saunders said that the JDF began to prepare a plan for Coke's arrest in January 2010. He said –

"Since the operation was to be joint with the JCF, they were fully involved."

3.26. Lt. Col. Andrew Sewell who commanded the Second Battalion of the Jamaica Regiment (2JR) returned from Moneague where 2JR had been on training exercises. He said that he became involved in planning for the operation in February 2010.

3.27. Lt. Col. Jaimie Ogilvie was the commanding officer of the First Battalion of the Jamaica Regiment (1JR). From the last week of August 2009, he was engaged in planning the operation to capture Coke. His first plan was presented at the end of September 2009 and was accepted. Further refinement of the plan continued through to December 2009, at which time he briefed CDS Saunders, Lt. Col. Sewell and CoP Ellington. In his witness statement, Lt. Col. Ogilvie said at para.9:

"Shortly before the New Year, I attended a meeting at HQ, JDF which was jointly chaired by the Commissioner of Police and the Deputy Chief of Defence Staff and including senior officers of the JDF and JCF. No operational plans were discussed but the meeting focused on guidance given by the Chairmen concerning the planning, processes and conduct of any operation to apprehend Mr Coke."

3.28. Lt. Col. Ogilvie stated that among the issues discussed and the guidance given –

"were the need to ensure that Mr Coke's rights were not violated, the rights of citizens were to be protected and the operation should consist of three phases – planning and preparation, search and capture, and the return to normalcy, the importance of examining past operations in Western Kingston, the need for disciplined but overwhelming force and the importance of the security forces having a positive impact on communities."

3.29. Between March and May 2010, 1JR did contingency planning, training and rehearsals. Emphasis was placed on the CDS's instructions for Opening Fire, Human Rights awareness, citizens' rights and issues such as span of control, de-confliction of unit boundaries, identification of friendly forces and the interpretation of the Emergency Powers Regulations were discussed and resolved.[32]

With both regular battalions of the Jamaica Regiment preparing for operations, the JCF made its own plans and it is still unclear as to how the two forces planned to work in synergy and as events would unfold, neither the JDF nor the JCF anticipated the level of resistance that they would face. Indeed, in respect of joint planning, the Commission of Inquiry noted:

3.30. We found rather disconcerting the evidence of CDS Saunders and CoP Ellington that neither knew of the other's plans, namely, OPERATION KEYWEST and OPERATION GARDEN PARISH. We do not believe that these were matters for secrecy at the highest was joint as between the two forces, the respective plans should have been seen and discussed certainly at the level of the respective Heads.[33]

One observation that was not made by the Commission of Inquiry was the issue of joint training for the operation. The JDF and JCF cooperate on a regular basis but it seems that neither force believed that they would face coordinated resistance, though there was a good understanding of the types of weapons available to Coke.

Prior to the beginning of the operation to seize Coke, Prime Minister Golding addressed the nation on 17 May 2010, apologised for his efforts to lobby the United States and questioned the evidence gathered in support of the United States' request for extradition. Golding apparently took both the JDF and JCF by surprise when he said, in announcing support and authorisation for the extradition to proceed:

This matter of the extradition has consumed too much of our energies and attention and has led to a virtual paralysis that must be broken…The nation's business cannot continue to be disrupted and distracted by the ordeal of the last several months.[34]

Apparently neither General Saunders nor Commissioner Ellington were informed of the decision to sign the authorisation to proceed and, as such, were completely taken by surprise. This was to prove costly as the Shower Posse was able to plan and mobilise.

The reaction in Tivoli Gardens was manifested in overt displays of support for Coke. Barricades began to be erected at the entrances of the neighbourhood and the Shower Posse began to mobilise and arm itself with an eclectic array of rifles and handguns and openly display these as they mounted patrols along the barricades.

Simultaneously, Coke mobilised the civilians of the neighbourhood, with whom he had cultivated a 'Robin Hood' type image. This led to a series of demonstrations which served to focus attention on the area. In addition, Coke mobilised other Jamaican gangs who sent armed supporters – perhaps 300 in all – to reinforce the Shower Posse. As the Commission of Inquiry noted:

> 3.44. Some 600 women, mainly dressed in white, took to the streets of West Kingston on 20 May demonstrating against execution of the warrant on Coke and pledging their loyalty to him. Placards exemplified the esteem in which these women held Coke: "Without Dudus, there will be no Jamaica"; "Next to God, Dudus"; "Jesus die for us, we will die for Dudus".
>
> 3.45. On the same day, the barricading and fortification of Tivoli Gardens were accelerated. The entrances to and the exits from the community were blocked. We were shown a large number of films and photographs of the blockading of Tivoli Gardens up to 23 May 2010. CoP Ellington's witness statement neatly encapsulates the nature of the barricading –
>
> "The barricades were constructed from old vehicles, old appliances, heavy equipment, scrap metal, sandbags and other solid materials. Several of the barricades had explosives embedded in them, with trigger mechanisms operable from inside residences. Road blocks were also mounted in other Corporate Area communities where gangs aligned to the Shower Posse had their bases."
>
> 3.46. We saw evidence of propane gas cylinders within the barricades and on a roadway. Barbed wire was used to block access to a street. Spanish Town Road was blockaded to prevent access to Tivoli Gardens. Near Darling Street, the access way to the community was heavily blocked. The sandbags referred to by CoP Ellington were used not only as blockade reinforcements but also as firing positions. The films and photographs, taken by the National Intelligence Bureau (NIB), captured images of men wearing bullet proof vests; men with night vision goggles; men piling sandbags; men with rifles and men keeping look out. Women were also seen watching the barricading in progress.
>
> 3.47. Fortification of Tivoli Gardens was swift and comprehensive. Intelligence available to the JCF and the JDF on a continuing basis was to the effect that, in the days leading up to 24 May, some 300 gunmen from all over Jamaica and loyal to Coke, had migrated into Tivoli Gardens and other parts of West Kingston. They had come to assist Coke and local gang members in resisting any attempt by the security forces to enter the Tivoli Gardens' community and arrest Coke.[35]

It was thus evident to both the JDF and JCF that they would face intense armed opposition from the Shower Posse and other gangs and that their foray into Tivoli Gardens would be fiercely resisted. The 1JR and 2JR (the first and second battalions of the Jamaica Regiment respectively) were assigned to support the JCF. 1JR was to establish a cordon around Tivoli Gardens, creating a buffer, while 2JR was assigned to actively support the JCF in apprehending Coke. Both battalions were fully mobilised and the remaining JDF V-150 armoured personnel carriers were assigned to support the respective battalions. In total, some 800 JDF personnel and 370 officers of the JCF were involved in the Tivoli Gardens incursion, with attendant support from other JDF and police units and with the full political backing of the government of the day. To date, Tivoli Gardens remains the JDF's biggest internal security operation.

The Tivoli Gardens gangs and their allies launched a series of attacks on the JCF with the aim of demoralising and/or deterring them from entering the neighbourhood. On 23 May 2010 alone, the following attacks were made:

> 5.30 a.m. Roadblocks mounted at the intersection of West Street and East Queen Street
>
> 7.58 a.m. Denham Town Police Station completely blocked in
>
> 8.04 a.m. Beckford Street and all roads leading to West Kingston blocked
>
> 6.30 a.m. Central units came under heavy gunfire while attempting to clear blockage
>
> 7.32 a.m. Industrial Terrace and Spanish Town road near Denham Town Primary School blocked
>
> 11.20 a.m. Darling Street Police report seeing men dressed in army fatigues, helmets and bullet proof vests in a blue building in Tivoli Gardens packing sandbags and placing large guns behind them
>
> 12.07 p.m. Police in Darling Street, Hannah Town and Denham Town Police Stations came under sustained gunfire
>
> 1.48 p.m. Police under heavy gunfire in Hannah Town, as reported by the rescue unit in the area. About 100 men were firing shots at the unit
>
> 1.58 p.m. Rescue 4 reports a police officer shot in Hannah Town and on his way to KPH
>
> 2.00 p.m. Hannah Town Police Station evacuated. Personnel and Government property removed
>
> 2.15 p.m. Police under heavy gunfire in West Street
>
> 2.59 p.m. The back of Hannah Town Police Station was on fire and the Fire Department was summoned
>
> 3.06 p.m. Report of armed men moving towards Trench Town Police Station
>
> 3.12 p.m. Police uniforms reported stolen from Hannah Town Police Station
>
> 3.18 p.m. Trench Town Police Station under heavy gunfire
>
> 3.22 p.m. Fletcher's Land Police Station under heavy gunfire
>
> 3.44 p.m. Rescue 4 under heavy gunfire at the intersection of Regent Street and Darling Street
>
> 4.13 p.m. Men seen on top of Flying Squad building with guns
>
> 4.13 p.m. Duke Street and North Street blocked
>
> 4.23 p.m. Denham Town Police Station bombe

4.35 p.m. Denham town Police Station under heavy gunfire and the police calling for help

5.47 p.m. SAC unit under gunfire at Slipe Pen Road; advised to retreat

6.10 p.m. Police advised to abandon their vehicle on Slipe Pen Road. It is taken over by criminals

6.52 p.m. and 7.36 p.m. Reports of attacks being planned for Vineyard Town Police Station and Central Village Police Station respectively

8.49 p.m. Maxfield Avenue and Spanish Town police under fire

8.54 p.m. Police under heavy gunfire at Sunrise Crescent near Red Hills Road

9.04 p.m. Fletcher's Land Police Station under heavy gunfire. Assistance sent

9.08 p.m. Report received that at 12.47 p.m. gunmen had invaded the Victoria Jubilee Hospital

9.12 p.m. A police vehicle crashed near that hospital. It is believed that the vehicle SAC 91 was stolen by criminals after it had been abandoned by its police occupants

9.50 p.m. Police attempt to clear road block at Flat Bridge and come under fire

11.37 p.m. PC Johnson's private vehicle was shot up in Perkins Boulevard

11.43 p.m. Police Officers in MPD 03 shot near Nannyville and the National Stadium

11.50 p.m. Police Corporal shot[36]

The JCF's Mobile Reserve, heavily armed and supplied with a number of armoured vehicles, was led at the time by Assistant Commissioner of Police Leon Rose. He led a team of 35 officers, with an APC in support to try to clear the barricades and regain control. However, in his own words:

> I saw a number of blockages of major streets – West Street; West Queen Street; Water Lane. On Industrial Terrace there was a barrage of gunfire coming from Tivoli Gardens and the Denham Town area near the Primary School. It sounded as though rifles were being fired. They were directed towards us, that is to say, towards Marcus Garvey Drive and Industrial Terrace. There was also gunfire from the vicinity of May Pen Cemetery. We had to turn back from Industrial Terrace. We could not clear the barricades. We had Intelligence that some of the barricades were booby-trapped. I heard on my radio that the team that was on its way to Denham Town police station could not proceed because of the intensity of the gunfire. The Commissioner and I were going from a different location than the team. They went from Spanish Town Road whereas we approached from Industrial Terrace. This was about 10.30 a.m.[37]

An APC at Hannah Town Police Station was severely damaged and had to be abandoned. Several police detachments were ambushed, leading to many casualties among the JCF personnel, with Constable Jason Davis being killed at 5:46 a.m. on 24 May 2010 and several JCF vehicles being destroyed or damaged.[38] The JDF was not immune from these attacks with their Up Park Camp being attacked on 23 May 2010 though the gunfire was described by Lieutenant Colonel David Cummings as being 'ineffective'.

The JCF and the JDF, after facing this onslaught, decided that they needed to take decisive action and at 8:00 a.m. on 24 May, the JDF soldiers of 1JR and 2JR and police officers, including members from the Mobile Reserve were assembled for briefings at Up Park Camp and Harmon Barracks, by their respective unit commanders. These briefings included detailed instructions on the use of force and the need to respect the human rights of the people in Tivoli Gardens. In addition, the commanders tried to lay down clear rules of engagement for the impending operation.[39]

Both JDF units – 1JR and 2JR – along with the JCF faced intense resistance as they moved by platoons into Tivoli Gardens. Captain Garth Anderson of 2JR stated:

> No.6 platoon encountered heavy resistance from gunmen located in the Coronation Market, inside the MPM building and on high-rise buildings located to the north of Tivoli Gardens in the vicinity of Tivoli Court. The gunmen were engaged with aimed controlled fire by members of the platoon. It is believed that these gunmen fled north towards the Denham Town community.[40]

The task of finding Coke and transporting him to a pre-determined location was assigned to Major Mahatma Williams and the Combat Support Battalion (CSB). His APCs (V-150s) and front end loader engineering vehicles were also tasked with clearing barricades. The CSB was also faced with sustained resistance and while its personnel were much better protected than those of 1JR and 2JR, they made extremely slow progress and the intensity and ability of their opposition surprised them. Major Williams deposed as follows:

> 30. There were multiple roadblocks; the first being at the railway crossing on Industrial Terrace. As the unit slowed down to allow the front end loader and APCs to clear the first blockage, a coordinated barrage of gunfire as per an ambush came from the Tivoli Gardens buildings off to our northeast and the open lot to the east.
>
> 31. Harassing gunfire was also coming from the direction of Universal Freight Handlers.
>
> 32. Overall, the bullets were mainly hitting the asphalt and a low wall to the east of us. Trees in the open lot were also being hit. The sandbags on the vehicles were hit and as a result their contents emptied out.
>
> 33. The firing from Universal Freight Handlers disrupted the movement of the support elements of the unit but was not significant enough to warrant being cleared. Up to this point my unit had suffered no casualties except for a few people who were suffering from heat related injuries.

> 34. The gunmen who had occupied Tivoli Gardens did not get the opportunity to detonate any explosives in the barriers where my unit manoeuvred.[41]

If this was not bad enough, the JDF received intelligence that one .50-inch anti-materiel rifle was available to the armed gangs in Tivoli Gardens. These weapons would have easily penetrated the lightly armoured V-150s of the JDF and the APCs of the JCF Mobile Reserve, not to mention the soft-skinned cars, jeeps and trucks of the security forces. Major Williams described the steps taken to protect the unarmoured JDF vehicles to the Commission of Inquiry, showing a commendable display of innovation and initiative:

> 18. We reinforced our patrol vehicles with sandbags strapped to the bonnets and dashboards so that the drivers had some degree of cover and also to protect the engines and radiators.
>
> 19. Our patrol vehicles were further fortified with bullet traps to make a barrier between the driver/commander in the front and the tail-end gunner. This was done to ensure that, if the driver were shot, the persons in the back of the vehicle would be able to continue fighting.[42]

Bravo Company of 1JR, under the command of Major Kevron Henry found itself facing intense resistance at Coronation Market, in the vicinity of the destroyed Darling Street police station. He found that the resistance was organised, determined and quite effective. Major Henry estimated that his unit took three hours to advance 500 metres, facing gunfire at every step of the way, with the resistance being extremely well coordinated.

Bravo Company's No.4 Platoon came under such heavy resistance that, at Foxy's Plaza, they took sufficiently heavy casualties that they were compelled to withdraw to prevent their own positions from being overrun. As the Commission of Inquiry noted:

> 4.82. The casualties suffered by No.4 platoon greatly retarded its progress and prevented the soldiers from securing the high ground of Foxy's Plaza which was critical to domination of the area. Maj. Henry told us that "securing the high ground of Foxy's Plaza would give the security forces watch over surrounding areas and various avenues of approach". It was imperative that this objective be achieved because the gunmen had forced the security forces along certain corridors and were manoeuvring in an orchestrated and preplanned manner "so as to create effective lanes and draw the security forces into kill zones."[43]

This impasse continued until 2nd Lieutenant D. Trowers used a V-150 APC to seize the nearby PassaPassa Plaza. The use of the V-150 provided sufficient protection to the troops to regain the initiative. Bravo Company gradually moved forward through the area and secured Foxy Plaza, PassaPassa Plaza and other key areas in the Coronation Market area. However, throughout the night of 24 May and into the early morning of 25 May, Bravo Company reported very intense gunfire with all section commanders reporting such incidents with attendant casualties. The JDF was faced with at least one .50-inch calibre Grizzly sniper rifle which, alongside rifle-calibre weapons, proved to be a major obstacle to their operations. The CSB was forced to deploy teams also equipped with .50-inch calibre sniper rifles to neutralise these opponents. The JCF did likewise but their rather more indiscriminate use of these weapons was not particularly useful.

Sporadic resistance continued all day of 25 May but the gunfire grew progressively less as the day went on. By 6:00 p.m. on 25 May, Bravo Company was finally able to secure the Denam Town area and, with the support of the JCF Mobile Reserve, was able to establish complete domination of the area. The 48 hours of fighting amply demonstrated the challenge that the JDF and JCF faced in dealing with the Tivoli Gardens gangs and was an ominous portent for future operations. The level of resistance encountered is partly reflected in the fact that some 115 weapons and over 15,000 rounds of ammunition were seized during the course of the operation, with only a fraction of the possible arsenal of the gang members being seized.

Over the next few days, the JDF and JCF found themselves having to clear out pockets of resistance. One of the more controversial aspects of the JDF's involvement was the decision to use 81mm mortars in urban terrain, the use of the said weapons being directly ordered by Chief of Defence Staff Saunders who explained his logic as follows:

> There was a need to keep women and children behind doors. Experience had shown that they were used as human shields. I needed the troops to have as much access as possible and to create a different sound in the operational area. They were fired under observed and controlled conditions. Each target was pre-determined and they were fired into three open areas. They had the desired effect. They created some disorientation and we never suffered many injuries and fatalities. There is no record of women and children killed during the operation. The mortars caused persons to remain behind doors.[44]

The mortars fired 37 rounds at three designated areas – the Seprod field, an open area near to the Community Centre in Tivoli Gardens and the football field on the eastern side of Tivoli Gardens – on 24 May 2010 and were under the command of Major Warrenton Dixon who was responsible for controlling the mortars and observing their impact. It has been suggested that alongside terrifying the civilians at Tivoli Gardens, two civilians were killed by the JDF's 81mm mortars.

The use of 81mm mortars was to prove extremely controversial and their use came in for scathing criticism, both at the time of the event and during a subsequent Commission of Inquiry which raised serious questions as to the judgement exercised by the CDS in authorising their use and the observation and controlling of the weapons by Major Dixon. The Commission stated:

> 10.175. Although we accept that two open playing fields were targeted for landing the mortars, we condemn the decision to explode mortars inside Tivoli Gardens itself. The area chosen was a heavily populated built-up area which carried a great risk of injury or death to residents. Our reading of materials provided by INDECOM on the use of mortars in international humanitarian law (IHL), convinces us that the weight of contemporary opinion, policy and law is against the use of mortars in densely populated areas, such as Tivoli Gardens. In the circumstances, we endorse the characterization by Maj. Cobb-Smith of the use of mortars within Tivoli Gardens, as "irresponsible and reckless".
>
> 10.187. We adhere to our finding that, notwithstanding the unprecedented and vicious attacks planned and executed by Coke and his gunmen, it was reckless and irresponsible to fire mortars within the community of Tivoli Gardens in circumstances where,

> on Maj. Dixon's own evidence, the safety distances were not respected. Their use within the community was disproportionate. With respect to the concept of proportionality, we note that the Constitution as it then was in 2010 did not incorporate proportionality as a restriction on fundamental rights and, in particular, the right to life. As such, it is doubtful whether Counsel for the JDF can properly rely on that concept in defence of their use of mortars.[45]

After two days of heavy fighting, the JDF and JCF were able to overcome most of the armed resistance but could not locate Coke who had gone into hiding. Coke's capture became a major priority for the JDF and JCF who were understandably chastened from their experience in the heavy fighting that occurred. The JDF's intelligence network, combined with the JCF's network of informants was able to track Coke and thus enable an interception of his vehicle on 22 June 2010 at which point he was detained and subsequently extradited to the United States.[46]

This was a somewhat anti-climactic end to a traumatic internal security operation for the Jamaican security and political establishments. The JCF could not have achieved any of its objectives without the support of the JDF which itself began to discover its own shortcomings in respect of training and equipment in the face of heavy resistance from well-armed gangs. This would lead to a subsequent re-equipment programme and an expansion of the Jamaica Regiment to cater for internal contingencies.

Despite the fact that the Tivoli Gardens incursion was ultimately successful, it was extremely costly. At least 73 bodies were recovered from Tivoli Gardens and the dead included one member of the JDF and three from the JCF. Some 30 soldiers and 28 police personnel were also injured in the fighting. Civilian deaths are estimated at 69, including those of up to 26 gang members.[47] The scale of the fighting is illustrated by the fact that this death toll is significantly higher than that sustained in Trinidad's Islamist insurrection of 1990, reflecting the security challenge of armed gangs.

The Jamaica Defence Force Today

Of all the forces being covered in this book, only the JDF has an active military reform programme which involves a combination of expansion and reorganisation. As the JDF itself phrases its objectives in respect of expansion and reorganisation:

> Significant and evolving activities in the global security environment have led to an increase in the size and commensurate structural reorganisation of the JDF. In that regard the Force is moving forward, in keeping with international doctrinal and military best practices and strategic analysis; in order to revamp its joint strategic headquarters, overall command structure and to also expand and rationalise its domain focused line entities.
>
> This revamped structure sees the Force increasing in size from a North Atlantic Treaty Organisation (NATO) standard Reinforced Brigade (Rein Bde) structure to that of a NATO standard combined arms Division (Div) structure. This combined arms Div structure is achieved through the revamp of the Joint/Div headquarters and the creation of four Brigade formations in addition to the Regimental size Jamaica National Service Corps (JNSC).
>
> These four (Bde) formations; three Regular Force (The Jamaica Regiment (Jca Regt), the Maritime, Air and Cyber Command (MACC) and the Support Brigade (Sp Bde)) in addition to an expanded Jamaica National Reserve (JNR) will task organise existing units along with the proposed new units/entities to provide the necessary operational oversight and management of the Force's capabilities in the land, air, sea and cyber domains. This overarching structure facilitates a greater focus by the Chief of Defence Staff and the Joint staff on matters of strategic importance to the Force, nation and region at large.[48]

Again, unique among armed forces of the English-speaking Caribbean, Jamaica has given some level of attention to establishing viable reserve forces and a cyber command. However, on the more negative side, Jamaica has placed less emphasis on its Coast Guard which is still relatively small and under resourced compared to the Jamaica Regiment. The JDF's Air Wing operates a very modern rotary wing component but its fixed wing assets have been severely depleted. In this regard, the Jamaica Defence Force is demonstrating its internal security priorities as the Jamaica Regiment has been called out repeatedly to assist the often beleaguered Jamaica Constabulary Force in anti-crime operations which turn violent.

Land Forces

From its original force, and one which persisted for a very long time, of two regular and one reserve battalions, the JDF land forces are being expanded to a very considerable extent. This may have been partly due to the events of Tivoli Gardens in 2010, which, as has been shown, was a traumatic event in Jamaica's military history as well as its internal security calculations. The JDF land forces are in the throes of a significant expansion of both its active and reserve formations and is on the path to becoming close to a small division in personnel strength.

The Jamaica Regiment – the land forces component of the JDF – describes itself and its strength in the following terms:

> The Jamaica Regiment is the operationalization of a terrestrial and combat focused Regular Force formation with an overarching operational headquarters in command of five (5) battalions; the First, Second, Fourth and Fifth Battalions the Jamaica Regiment (1, 2, 4, 5 JR) and the Combat Support Battalion (Cbt Sp Bn).[49]

Table 14: JDF strength

	Strength
Active personnel	Approx. 4,000
Reserves	Approx. 1,500

The land component of the Jamaica Defence Force (JDF) is the Jamaica Regiment, which fields three regular infantry battalions with at least one more being created. These units have mostly light arms but also operate the support weapons in the JDF inventory. The JDF created Geographic Commands to allow its formations to cover a wider area of the country:

> The ever evolving and increasing security concerns that affects Jamaica overtime has led to a complete restructuring and rationalization of the Jamaica Defence Force (JDF) in an effort to optimise the use of resources. This optimisation includes the creation of three (3) Geographic Commands that will conduct infantry operation in those specific areas covering the entire Island.

Bushmaster APCs of the Jamaica Regiment on patrol. (JDF)

Bushmasters exiting their base. (JDF)

The creation of these Geographic Commands necessitates the need for a third Regular Force Infantry Battalion to support The First Battalion The Jamaica Regiment (1 JR) and The Second Battalion The Jamaica Regiment (2 JR). To satisfy this requirement the Defence Board, on 15 May 2018 gave approval for the establishment of The Fourth Battalion The Jamaica Regiment (4 JR).[50]

The Regular Force, which now includes the 5 JR, also has a Support and Services Battalion, a Combat Support Battalion – which has the Protected Mobility Vehicle Squadron with its Bushmaster APCs – and an Engineer Regiment. The primary role of the JDF is to defeat or deter violence threatening the nation state and its people. While this includes the defence of the country against terrorism and external aggression, in practice it mostly undertakes counter-narcotics and anti-crime operations which have often required the mobilisation of the National Reserve.[51]

Jamaica's army is designed to be multipurpose, being able to provide national defence as well as internal security, with many of its missions geared towards counter-narcotics. The deployment of the Jamaica Regiment alongside and supporting the police to curb drug trafficking and violent crime has also increased in recent years, giving it an enhanced internal security profile. However, in this context, only police officers have legal powers of search and arrest.

Meanwhile, the Jamaica Regiment has limited conventional military capabilities but joint training exercises with a variety of foreign countries – mainly the US and UK – maintain a reasonable level of infantry skills.[52]

As has been discussed, the JR operated a significant force of V-150 APCs – the figure of 15 being most cited. However, the bulk of the army's LAV-150 commando armoured personnel carriers, which were acquired in the 1970s, were not roadworthy by the early 2000s and were in dire need of repair or replacement, with only three being operational in 2009.[53]

With this in mind, the JDF in late 2013 signed a contract with Thales Australia for 12 Bushmaster 4x4 protected mobility vehicles. The vehicles are troop carrier variants equipped with Thales' SOTAS M2 multimedia communications system, a Caterpillar 3126E diesel engine, ZF 6HP502 ECOMAT G2 automatic transmission, W&E Platt machine gun ring, and provisions for government furnished communications. Deliveries began in March 2015, when the first three vehicles were delivered. Another three vehicles were delivered in November, and deliveries were completed in January 2016. A five-year support package is included in the contract. The JDF was well pleased with the Bushmaster and in 2020 a contract for a further six vehicles was placed.

Table 15: Details of JDF Bushmaster APCs

Type	Role	In service	First delivery
Bushmaster	Tactical/light utility	12 and 6 on order	2015

The Bushmaster APCs are in service with the Protected Mobility Squadron of the Combat Support Battalion. This CSB is described as:

> The vision of the Combat Support Battalion (Cbt Sp Bn) is to provide for the JDF a composite operational unit, equipped with the dynamic requisite skills, knowledge and attitudes for deterring threats against Jamaica in all types and stages of operations.

Two Bushmaster of the Jamaica Regiment. (JDF)

V-150 armoured car of the Jamaica Regiment. (JDF)

> Through the exercise of mission command, the Cbt Sp Bn will exercise flexibility in its planning, supervision and execution of operations in support of the Jamaica Regiment, thereby allowing the combined security forces the ability to secure the Jamaican populace and their legitimate interests…
>
> The Combat Support Battalion is now the Chief of Defence Staff's operational flexibility and manoeuvre element, allowing for mechanized infantry support to be made available in any operational area across Jamaica. It is currently the home of the Protected Mobility Vehicle Squadron, made up of the Caribbean's first and currently only fleet of Bushmaster Thales vehicles. The mechanized infantry allows for the movement of troops under protection in order to render assistance of varied forms to light infantry and other military units. The Unit provides this capability to units deployed across the island, with particular focus currently on assisting the Jamaica Constabulary Force with the conduct of internal security operations.[54]

A less glamourous but more important modernisation programme was undertaken with infantry equipment, as L1A1 SLRs and British pattern web-gear and helmets were replaced with US-made M16 rifles, M249 SAWs and US pattern helmets, woodland camouflage and web-gear. This switch to US pattern equipment has been quite widespread and has also affected the Jamaica Constabulary Force which now is also largely American armed.

The Jamaica Regiment also maintains a substantial support brigade which is a Regular Force, as opposed to a National Reserve, formation that enables the provision of both combat support and service support functions. The Support Brigade is the operational headquarters for four units: the Support and Services Battalion (Sp and Svcs Bn), 1 Engineer Regiment JDF (1 Engr Regt (JDF)), the Health Services Corps (HSC) and the Corps of Military Police (CMP).[55] Of these, the Sp and Svcs Bn has a strength of 20 officers and 700 other ranks, arranged into eight companies.

The 1 Engineering Regiment JDF is a recently created formation and provides civil and military support:

> 1 Engineer Regiment (JDF) was formed in August 1991 and became fully operational on 01 April 1992. Prior to this all military and civil engineering tasks were carried out by two sub-units under command of the Support and Services Battalion: the JDF Construction Squadron and the JDF Engineer Unit. An increase in national demand for military engineers led Headquarters JDF to seek and obtain the approval of the Government to form the Engineer Regiment.[56]

The National Reserve

The JDF's National Reserve is officially described as:

> The Jamaica National Reserve (JNR) is a multi-domain focused reserve force formation that has been expanded to include a headquarters element in command of four (4) units; the Third, Sixth and Ninth Battalions the Jamaica Regiment (3, 6 and 9 JR (NR)) in addition to the Support Battalion (National Reserve) (Sp Bn (NR).[57]

In practice, the National Reserve is an infantry force with each battalion comprising six companies, with a small number of Regular Force personnel attached to each NR battalion.

The Maritime, Air and Cyber Command

Rather surprisingly, Jamaica has opted to group its Coast Guard and Air Wing into an umbrella unit called the Maritime, Air and Cyber Command (MACC). While the Cyber category is as yet nascent and now finding itself a role as a viable unit in the form of the Military Cyber Corps. The Air Wing of the JDF and the Coast Guard are small units compared to the Jamaica Regiment and it is perhaps in recognition of this that these two formations have been subsumed under the MACC. The MACC is officially described by the JDF website as follows:

> The Maritime, Air and Cyber Command (MACC) is a multi-domain focused Regular Force formation with an operational headquarters in command of six (6) units; the First and Second Districts Jamaica Defence Force Coast Guard (1st and 2nd Dist JDF CG), the Jamaica Defence Force Air Wing (JDF AW), the Military Intelligence Unit (MIU), the Special Activities Regiment (SPEAR) and the Military Cyber Corps (MCC).[58]

The MIU and SPEAR are two units without effective parallel within the Caribbean and possess capabilities commensurate with their functions within resource constraints.

Air Wing

Table 16: JDF Air Wing strength

	Strength
Active personnel	200*
Reserves	15

* Sanctioned strength as of 2009 was 189.

Jamaica's Defence Force (JDF) Air Wing is also undergoing modernisation with its helicopter fleet being extensively modernised with new, more modern, Bell helicopters while a limited recapitalisation of its fixed wing fleet is being undertaken as additional maritime patrol assets are being sought.

The JDF Air Wing has no conventional military capabilities and its capability to undertake even support missions is limited. The service's BN2 has been withdrawn from use and is a ground instruction platform, while the new DA40/42s are primarily training assets with a secondary surveillance role. The Bell 412 and the Bell 407s are the principal SAR assets. Given the size of the country's EEZ and the regional issues with drug trafficking, the fleet is insufficient to provide the required SAR and EEZ patrol requirements. Nevertheless, it is sufficient to provide minimum level SAR in the direct vicinity of the island.

The JDF Air Wing has been dependent until quite recently on outside agencies for the provision of training, although this is increasingly being undertaken within the country, following the creation of a small training establishment in 2006 with Canadian assistance. The establishment of training schools for both fixed and rotary wing units – the Diamond aircraft for the former and the Bell 206 for the latter – will stand the JDF Air Wing in good stead in the future. The JDF is therefore alone among the armed forces of the English-speaking Caribbean in that it is able to provide a comprehensive level ab initio training for its pilots. This is despite the fact that the JDF Air Wing has only a single fixed wing aircraft. Any expansion of the fixed wing assets of the JDF, therefore, will find the service in good shape to provide trained personnel for its requirements.

Rotary Wing Assets

The JDF Air Wing's Rotary Assets are in No.2 Flight of the force. This Flight is an all-Bell outfit at present as the JDF's Air Wing, as noted earlier, has a long and very productive relationship with Bell. There was a brief interlude when a force of Eurocopter AS.355s were procured in the 1990s but Jamaica was to return to the Bell family in the twenty-first century when it would operate no fewer than four variants of Bell helicopters. None of the JDF's helicopters are armed. However, their helicopters have been used extensively in internal security operations, with some legislative measures becoming necessary to allow JDF and JCF snipers to fire from the aircraft during operations in urban environments. As with much of the JDF inventory, the Air Wing went through serviceability crises in the early 2000s.

The JDF Air Wing currently operates a mixed fleet of Bell 206s, Bell 407s, Bell 412s and Bell 429s. The fleet now has but a single Bell 206, two 412s and three Bell 407s of variable operational serviceability. However, the JDF is intent on phasing out all its Bell 407s and 412s in favour of a modern, uniform fleet of nine Bell 429s.[59] Lieutenant Colonel Brian Lundy, of No.2 Flight stated:

> When we assessed our operations, we realized that with the 206, the 407, the 412, that was already three different platforms that we had to maintain and get parts for … But having looked at what we need to do for the country, we have now decided to maintain two types. The Bell 206 that we use for training, and the Bell 429 which we use for everything else.[60]

The nine JDF Bell 429s are built to civilian specifications, with no militarisation being undertaken. But, in recognition of their purpose, the aircraft are equipped to carry Goodrich hoists and, for surveillance operations, are also fitted with Trakka Systems TrakkaBeam searchlights and Wescam MX-10 Gen-IV cameras. For the deployment of special forces, the aircraft are also fitted with fast-roping and rappelling equipment. As with many helicopters in the Caribbean, for firefighting missions, a 260-gallon (1,000-litre) Bambi Bucket from SEI Industries can be slung under the aircraft.[61]

The JDF Bell 429s will be the best equipped helicopters in the Caribbean but their capacity is significantly lower than the Bell 412s that they will eventually replace. This is deemed to be an acceptable risk as Lieutenant Colonel Lundy indicated that the new technology of the aircraft will make the investment worthwhile: 'Transitioning from the 412 to the 429, we get a nice glass cockpit, so what we have now is top of the line'. He reserved particular praise for the aircraft's four-axis automatic flight control system (AFCS): 'The automation is fantastic. When we went to the drawing board to decide what we needed based on the amount of over-water work, we wanted to ensure that pilot workload was reduced. So, all of our aircraft will have the four-axis autopilot.'[62]

In addition, a force of six Bell 505s is replacing the Bell 206s. This would ensure a homogeneity in the fleet that would aid in its long-term sustainability and maintainability. This is assisted by the fact that the Bell 505 and the Bell 429 will have a certain degree of commonality. These aircraft will also be used to train pilots throughout the Caribbean while augmenting the Bell 429s for internal security operations and in support of both the JDF and the JCF. Bell's press release stated:

> With a speed of 125 knots (232 kilometers per hour) and useful load of 1,500 pounds (680 kilograms), the Bell 505 is Bell's newest five-seat aircraft designed for safety, efficiency and reliability

Beech King Air 350R of the JDF Air Wing. (JDF)

Table 17: Jamaica Defence Force Air Wing Current Assets

Platform family	Platform variant	Primary role (general)	Primary role (specific)	Estimated in service	First delivery date
Beech King Air	350 WR		Maritime Surveillance	1	2018
DA40 Diamond Star	DA40	Trainer	Basic	2	2006
DA42 Twin Star	DA42	Trainer	Basic	2	2009
Bell 412	Bell 412EP	Logistics	Utility	2*	1998
Bell 206			Training	1	
Bell 407	407	Surveillance	Utility	3**	2007
Bell 429		Surveillance and Logistics		7 with 2 on order	

* H-23 and H-25 are in service. H-23 was repaired after an 8-year gap.
** H-31 is damaged (since July 2007 and in storage). This leaves three in service – H-30, H-32 and H-33.

> using advanced avionics technology. Its similarities with the Bell 429 platform allow for a smooth pilot transition as JDF begins training operations. With a Garmin G1000, the platform shares similar avionics with JDF's Fixed Wing Trainer aircraft and reduces pilot workload, enhancing the students' learning experience.[63]

The mix of Bell 429s, with their surveillance equipment, and the Bell 505s in support will give the JDF a good level of air support within the requirement of their internal security framework. The Bell 429s may also prove to be reasonably effective maritime patrol and Search and Rescue Assets but they cannot carry out long-range patrols and are not equipped to undertake anything more than limited surveillance and patrol missions. For such tasks, the JDF requires an adequate force of fixed wing assets and it is in this regard that the JDF Air Wing has fallen on hard times with its inventory now reduced to a handful of aircraft with one tasked with maritime surveillance and patrol.

Fixed Wing Assets

Aside from the two DA 40 Diamond Star and two DA 42 Twin Star ab initio flying trainers, and one Beech King Air 350, the JDF Air Wing is in dire need of fixed wing assets. While the Twin Star can carry three passengers, the JDF has not found replacements for nor has aggressively sought such replacement for its once considerable fleet of Cessna, De Havilland Canada, Rockwell Commander, Beech King Air and BN-2 Islander aircraft. The fact is that the JDF has no viable transport aircraft and can no longer move either troops or cargo by air beyond the ability of its helicopter fleet.

The JDF's sole viable and modern fixed wing asset is a single Beech King Air 350 WR obtained in 2018. This aircraft is equipped with intelligence, surveillance and reconnaissance (ISR) equipment.[64] There are suggestions that the JDF may be intent on acquiring a second as part of its efforts to build its maritime surveillance assets, which include the acquisition of four additional Damen patrol vessels.[65]

Jamaica Coast Guard

The Jamaican Coast Guard underwent a period of uncertainty and varying fortunes in the first decade of the 21st century. In the period 2004–2006, the Coast Guard fleet was rejuvenated with three Damen SPa 4207 patrol craft and two ageing patrol boats HMJS *Fort Charles* and HMJS *Paul Bogle* refitted by Damen. The rest of the fleet consisted of old US-made Dauntless-class patrol boats and a number of interceptor craft and *Boston Whaler* type vessels. By 2012, the fleet was composed of the assets shown in Table 18.

However, because the JDF failed to procure spares beyond the warranty period, compounded by the country's poor economic condition, the fleet soon fell into disrepair. HMJS *Fort Charles* was decommissioned in 2012 and the other vessels were almost completely unserviceable with HMJS *Paul Bogle* being decommissioned in 2020 after a prolonged period of inactivity.[66] The three Damen SPa 4207s were virtually inoperable by 2012 though they were nominally still in commission.

Table 18: Jamaica Coast Guard vessels			
Name of Ship	**Length**	**Builder**	**Delivery**
HMJS *Cornwall*	42.8m	Damen Group	2006
HMJS *Middlesex*	42.8m	Damen Group	2006
HMJS *Surrey*	42.8m	Damen Group	2007
HMJS *Fort Charles* (P 7)	35.3m	Swiftships	1974
HMJS *Paul Bogle* (P 8)	32.3m	Lantana Boatyard	1985
Source: Jamaica Defence Force Website			

Table 19: Jamaica Coast Guard personnel strength	
	Strength
Active personnel	340 (estimated based on 2010 figures)
Reserves	50

In 2015, however, Jamaica concluded a peculiar deal with Damen whereby its three Damen SPa 4207s would be decommissioned and returned to Damen in exchange for two new SPa 4207s that Damen had in stock. The decommissioning and return of the JDF vessels took place on 8 November 2016 and it was intended, after refurbishment, to offer them for resale.[67] The two replacement vessels were named (after their predecessors) HMJS *Cornwall* and HMJS *Middlesex* and after undergoing modification and outfitting were delivered to the JDF in 2016. It should be noted that these vessels have an austere equipment suite and lack advanced surveillance systems or weapons larger than machine guns. However, the SPa 4207 is a cost-effective solution to Jamaica's maritime patrol needs and, like many other countries in the Western Hemisphere, Jamaica has decided to continue using the type. The two vessels now form the primary assets of the Jamaican Coast Guard and provide the country's sole ability to patrol its maritime domain.

The Jamaica Coast Guard, therefore, after its expansion, had the personnel strength shown in Table 19.

The Jamaica Defence Force (JDF) Coast Guard is tasked with mainly coastal internal security and maritime law enforcement missions, in addition to maritime safety tasks (primarily search and rescue). The core of its fleet is formed around the two aforementioned two Damen Stan Patrol 4207 patrol craft.

The Jamaican Coast Guard's ability to wage conventional combat operations is non-existent, but it can operate at the lower end of the force spectrum. The Damen Stan Patrol 4207s gave the coast guard the ability to undertake and sustain extended operations throughout its Exclusive Economic Zone, something its smaller and older patrol craft could not provide. After 2016, the two new Damen Stan Patrol 4207s have not met the fate of their predecessors and have continued to function in service with a very high degree of serviceability and availability for missions.

Also of importance, the JDF Coast Guard's interceptor craft provide it with the ability to interdict go-fast vessels. That said, maintenance and spare parts are an ongoing problem, with a significant proportion of the small fleet out of operation at any one time. The capability was recently boosted through the donation of five Boston Whaler 37ft patrol vessels and five SAFE (secure all-around flotation equipped) boats, delivered over a number of years ending in 2019, as gifts from the United States.[68]

New Damen SPa 4207 vessel of the Jamaica Coast Guard. (Damen Shipyards)

FCS 5009-class *Nanny of the Maroons* of the Jamaica Coast Guard. (JDF)

HMJS *Cornwall* and HMJS *Middlesex*. (Damen Shipyards)

Jamaica's older fleet of interceptors, however, is of varying serviceability and has not been without problems of maintenance and product support and it is questionable as to whether any of the older vessels are still in service. The close relationship the JDF Coast Guard maintains with the United States has enabled the Coast Guard to replace its force of interceptors that are of two principal types which, together with the procurement of a supply of spare parts, should ensure their serviceability in the short to medium term.

The Jamaica Coast Guard participates in exercise Tradewinds, which is organised by US SOUTHCOM and which is a necessary tool to promote regional cooperation and provide training to Caribbean security forces to address drug trafficking, organised crime, human and weapons trafficking, and illegal fishing. However, the JDF Coast Guard is still one of the weaker ones in the region – being much smaller than either the Trinidad or Bahamas units. Of note, current plans call for the coast guard to grow its personnel strength to around 450.

The Jamaica Defence Force (JDF) contracted Damen Shipyards Group to build two new Stan Patrol 4207 vessels to replace the core of the JDF Coast Guard's fleet, which consisted of three vessels of the same type. The old vessels were decommissioned in November 2016

Table 20: Jamaica Coast Guard Current Fleet

Class	Manufacturer	Role	In service	Commissioned
County (Damen Stan Patrol 4207)	Damen Shipyard	Patrol craft	2 and 2 on order	2017
Damen FCS 5009	Damen Shipyard	Patrol craft	1 and 1 on order	2020
Dauntless	SeaArk Marine	Patrol craft – inshore	4	1992 (doubtful serviceability)
Fast Coastal Interceptors	Silver Ships Theodore	Patrol craft – fast	3	2003 (doubtful serviceability)
Fast Coastal Interceptors	Nor-Tech	Patrol craft – fast	4	2008 (doubtful serviceability)
6m Fast Patrol Boat	Boston Whaler	Patrol craft – fast	1	2008 (doubtful serviceability)
9m Fast Patrol Boat	Boston Whaler	Patrol craft – fast	1	2008 (doubtful serviceability)
Justice	Boston Whaler	Patrol craft – fast	5	2015
SAFE International	Secure all-around flotation equipped	Patrol craft – fast	5	2015

Another view of the HMJS *Cornwall* and HMJS *Middlex*. (Damen Shipyards)

HMJS *Nanny of the Maroons* at sea. (Damen Shipyards)

and the new ones, HMJS *Cornwall* and HMJS *Middlesex*, entered service in March 2017.[69] The core responsibility of the patrol fleet will remain monitoring Jamaica's Exclusive Economic Zone, and cracking down on illegal fishing, drug trafficking and weapons smuggling.

Subsequently, the JDF Coast Guard moved to place further orders with Damen for two more SPa 4207 patrol boats and two FCS 5009 vessels.[70] One of the latter vessels, now named *Nanny of the Maroons* has been commissioned.[71] Jamaica has, like many other Caribbean countries, chosen to place its trust in Damen vessels but has not opted to equip them with advanced equipment but has rather chosen to follow a path of cost-effectiveness and limited though adequate weaponry for the constabulary role.

Jamaica has also invested – like Trinidad and Barbados – in a comprehensive coastal radar network. However, unlike the latter two countries, Jamaica has not opted for an Elta system but rather for a network based around the Thales Coast Watcher radar. Under a US$ 100 million contract, Jamaica Defence Force (JDF) will be provided with a turnkey system that centres around a series of Coast Watcher 100 radars, electro-optical sensors, and Global Maritime Distress and Safety System (GMDSS) radios. These will be integrated with a National Control Centre to provide data fusion from these sensors.[72]

In 2019, the Jamaica Coast Guard was divided into two districts – the 1st District and the 2nd District. At present, the 1st District possesses most of the fleet's holding but it is expected that when the remaining Damen vessels are delivered, the 2nd District will receive a full inventory of viable patrol assets.

Conclusion

Compared to the defence forces of Trinidad and Tobago and the Commonwealth of the Bahamas, the JDF confronts similar security threats in the maritime sphere and from narcotics trafficking. Like Trinidad, it also faces a difficult internal security environment with its forces being deployed to augment a beleaguered police force against well-armed organised gangs. However, the JDF faces these challenges with the spectre of having to rely on a weak Jamaican economy to support its requirements. To the credit of the JDF and Jamaica, decisions have been made and resources allocated to keep the force viable in the years to come. Nonetheless, this viability will be contingent on adequate budgetary support being made available for the maintenance and upkeep of JDF assets and it remains to be seen if this will be forthcoming in the future.

6

TRINIDAD AND TOBAGO DEFENCE FORCE

The Trinidad and Tobago Defence Force (TTDF) is perhaps the most experienced unit in the English-speaking Caribbean. In 1990, it successfully quelled an Islamist insurrection which held the then government hostage. Prior to that, it suffered the ignominy of a mutiny in 1970. Today, despite being one of the larger forces in the region, it is suffering from a severe crisis of asset availability with an attendant dramatic decline in combat efficacy. The TTDF, however, has been increasingly seen as an asset to support the beleaguered police service in a battle against criminal gangs and while its deployment is quite heavy, investment in enhancing its capabilities is very limited.

Trinidad and Tobago

Trinidad and Tobago lies at the southernmost point of the Caribbean Archipelago, only 11km off the coast of north-east Venezuela. Trinidad and Tobago is an industrialised society with a high literacy rate and large petrochemical, petroleum and natural gas sectors. Literacy exceeds 98 percent and education up to tertiary level is free.[1] While there is income disparity and some level of deprivation, Trinidad's per capita income is no less than US$ 21,000 in nominal terms with a very high human development index.[2]

Demographically, the country has a stable population of just over 1.3 million, with 35.4 percent of the population being of

Indian origin, 34.2 percent of African descent and 22.8 percent of mixed parentage.[3] In terms of religion, 57 percent of the population identifies itself as Christian, 18 percent as Hindu and 13 percent as having no religion. Adherents to the Islamic faith comprise only 5 percent of the population.[4]

Security Challenges

The growth of the North American cocaine market in the 1980s was to see a total transformation of the narcotics landscape in the country. While cocaine addiction began to increase – young Afro-Trinidadians being among the worst affected[5] – the country itself became a major cocaine trans-shipment point for cocaine originating in South America for onward progression to the United States,[6] aided by border surveillance, corruption and judicial and bureaucratic inertia.

Trinidad thus found itself confronted with an increase in narcotics shipments through its territory and a major increase in the number of addicts emerging in the urban communities. In addition, with the cocaine trade came the first major inflow of illegal firearms into the country.[7] Hitherto, few weapons were smuggled in and even those were handguns for criminals. The cocaine trade brought with it a new level of arms smuggling, largely of handguns, once again, but increasingly a small trickle of rifles and shotguns began finding their way into the hands of criminal elements who began to display increasing brazenness.[8]

More recently, the nexus between Islamic extremism, terrorist groups and organised crime has emerged a major and as yet insurmountable challenge. In 2015, no fewer than 35 Trinidadians were identified as fighting for ISIS with other family members supporting them, actively bringing the total to 89.[9] By 2016, this figure may well have been an underestimate as figures discussed in Trinidad's Parliament placed the numbers at anywhere between 102 and a staggering 400.[10] Trinidadian police intelligence suggests that between 10 and 15 Trinidadians have been killed fighting for ISIS so far, although reliable information is difficult to obtain.[11]

Trinidadians became 'poster boys' for an ISIS recruiting video made in late 2015 which included their children.[12] Indeed, in the said video, one identifying himself as Abu Zayd al-Muhajir had brought his three children to Syria in the Ar-Raqqah province while another – Abu Khalid, a Christian convert – used the video to proclaim that Muslims in Trinidad were 'restricted'. This was echoed by Zayd al-Muhajir and yet another Trinidadian, Abu Abdullah, who went so far as to encourage Muslims in Trinidad to support ISIS and its ambition of creating an Islamic Caliphate with some limited success.

Trinidad is also plagued by an epidemic of violent crime where well-organised gangs vie for control of inner-city areas and the very lucrative narcotics trade enables them to procure large quantities of weapons. Many of these gangs, it is to be noted, who are affiliated with Islamic extremist groups, have secured control over whole swathes of Port of Spain, the capital city, and have begun to expand their zones of influence and control. With private armies nearly the size of infantry battalions, they have begun to exert their power further afield, targeting the populous urban and semi-urban communities. The police have been largely ineffective in controlling these gangs.

The Trinidad and Tobago Police Service (TTPS), on 13 February 2017, had a sanctioned strength of 7,884 full-time officers with an 'actual strength' at that date of 6,768, a 14 percent or 1,116 deficit, and should in theory be able to exert control and authority over gang-controlled territory. In addition, the TTPS has support in the form of the Special Reserve Police (SRP) which were supposed to be a reserve force but some 2,496 are employed on a full-time basis with only 652 being part-time. Furthermore, the TTPS is well-armed with assault rifles and submachine guns and is well-supplied with vehicles. However, the TTPS, despite being well paid, is plagued by incompetence, corruption, lethargy and extreme levels of inefficiency which has left a large proportion of its vehicles unserviceable. Compounding this is an ineffective shift system that ensures that only 23 percent of the total strength of the TTPS is available on any given day. This unfortunate combination of factors has ensured that whole swathes of territory fall under the sway of criminal gangs. Into this internal security mess, the TTDF has been asked to participate in many joint patrols.

The Organisational Set-up

Trinidad and Tobago does not have a separate Ministry of Defence. All security matters, plus the fire services and passport control and immigration, are handled by the Ministry of National Security. Control of this Ministry is vested in the Minister of National Security who, as a member of the country's cabinet, is responsible to the Prime Minister.

The Minister of National Security is usually not a subject matter specialist and relies heavily on the advice of the leaders of the country's protective services. This also extends to the bureaucracy that is responsible for the day-to-day affairs of the Ministry, responsible for allocations, releasing funds for repairs and stores, and to clearing procurement. In a practical sense, the Ministry is run by its bureaucrats with the Minister having no power to hold them accountable.

The Trinidad and Tobago Defence Force is operationally controlled by the Chief of Defence Staff who in turn reports to the Minister of National Security but is not under the latter's operational direction. This preserves a relatively apolitical nature of the military. However, the Chief of Defence Staff has very limited powers and has little practical control over force development or structure as the latter has to be subject to financial approvals as well as to conform to the political wishes of the government of the day. This can prove to be a frustrating experience for any progressive thinking CDS.

The TTDF is under the control of the Minister of National Security who is in turn a member of the National Security Council. Directly under the Minister of National Security is the Defence Council and the Chief of Defence Staff in turn is nominally subordinate to the Defence Council.[13] In reality the Defence Council rarely functions and then only for a limited number of issues leaving the CDS to report to the Minister of National Security as needed and where necessary to the Prime Minister through the National Security Council.

It should be noted that while the CDS does have considerable administrative authority, its practical powers are limited to matters of force administration with very limited financial powers. The CDS has little to no input into overall national security policy which is largely the purview of the Minster of National Security under the direction of the Prime Minister. This means that while the CDS is consulted on major issues, his input is not usually decisive and not necessarily taken into full account in the development of policies.

The Trinidad and Tobago Police Service was and is a much more visible entity as might be expected and is under the administrative and operational control of the Commissioner of Police. The Commissioner of Police is probably the single most powerful yet most difficult post in the national security structure as the Commissioner is held responsible, by the public and by politicians for every increase in crime or criminality and also has to grapple with a dysfunctional procurement system which precludes timely replacement or repairs to existing systems leading to a very low level of operational efficiency and poor efficacy.

The Trinidad and Tobago Defence Force

The Trinidad and Tobago Defence Force (TTDF) was formed in 1962 prior to the country's gaining of independence from the United Kingdom. The TTDF, as established, had a land-based element – the Trinidad and Tobago Regiment (TTR), and a naval element – the Trinidad and Tobago Coast Guard (TTCG). A small reserve force called the Volunteer Defence Force (VDF) was also established.

The TTR was established as a battalion sized outfit while the TTCG was established with a modest personnel strength but with two capable patrol boats.

A BRIEF HISTORY OF THE TTDF

The Federation Experiment

The Trinidad and Tobago Defence Force emerged out of an unsuccessful, but ambitious plan, to create a military force encompassing the whole English-speaking Caribbean, as described in the chapter on Jamaica. The failure of the Federation meant that local military forces needed to be established by the individual countries.

For Trinidad and Jamaica, with the dates for their declarations of independence set for August 1962, the need became acute as it became necessary to break up the existing, albeit very small, units of the West India Regiment. This enabled the formation of the defence forces of Jamaica, Barbados and Trinidad.

The Birth of the TTDF

Unlike Jamaica, and to a large extent Barbados, which had a long established and proud military tradition, and one which was maintained assiduously even after the end of the Second World War, the Trinidad Regiment had been disbanded in 1947 and its colours stored in Trinity Cathedral, Port of Spain.[14] The men of the Trinidad Regiment, by 1962, had aged considerably and were not fit for re-engagement in a military force, even if they had wanted to, as many had gone on into the civil service and the professions with considerable success and corresponding financial reward.

A new Trinidad and Tobago Regiment had to be forged and to this end Major, later Lieutenant Colonel, Peter Pearce-Gould, was to oversee the recruitment of officer cadets for the new military force. He recruited, among others, Major Stewart Hylton-Edwards who was to rise to become a company commander in the new TTR, and selected one Major Joffre Serrette, a Trinidadian who had served in the part-time Trinidad Volunteers before rising to the rank of staff-sergeant before being commissioned. Serrette had no operational experience and had only held administrative positions but was being groomed to become the Trinidadian commanding officer.

It should be noted that when the Trinidadian Minister of Home Affairs, Dr Patrick Solomon, announced to the country's Prime Minister, Dr Eric Williams, that he had re-established the Trinidad and Tobago Regiment with some seconded officers and NCOs and others from the disbanded West India Regiment, the Prime Minister was taken aback stating that he had never asked for a regiment but wanted instead a 'National Guard'.[15] The plan for the regiment, such as it was, was to replace the police service's paramilitary functions, allowing the latter to become a largely unarmed civil force.

From the outset, realising that Trinidad would not be able to afford a large military force, the land element was to consist of a single infantry battalion with three rifle companies to which it was

Dingo armoured cars of the TTR. (TTR)

Shorland APCs of the TTR. (Photo by Author)

planned to add later three volunteer rifle companies as a reserve.[16] The force would be led by a lieutenant colonel who, for reasons of economy, would also be the commander of the entire TTDF. The TTDF would consist of a single infantry battalion and a coast guard with a modest force of patrol boats. There was no air element initially envisaged for the TTDF though the need for a modest liaison and patrol aircraft capability was appreciated and would eventually emerge prior to 1970.

The initial batch of officers was recruited from an eclectic mix of civil servants, teachers, businessmen and immigration officers, many of whom had no military experience.[17] This would later become a source of friction as a new generation of Sandhurst trained junior officers would emerge and question the competence of their less qualified superiors. Nevertheless, the TTDF was established successfully and was able to assume its duties as a ceremonial force and as a support for the police service as required. The TTDF was never envisaged as being capable of being a force capable of defending the country against a major adversary but it was expected to be capable of internal counter-insurgency and operations in support of the police against rioting workers or left-wing agitations.

Training and Composition

As noted, there was considerable difficulty in recruiting qualified officers. This was gradually ameliorated as more and more Trinidadian cadets were sent to officer training academies overseas. A rather more serious problem was the lack of an officer 'caste' and a problem with the non-commissioned officers being unwilling to take responsibility for the often harsh and uncompromising, but scrupulously fair discipline that must perforce be part of any military force. These issues were particularly noticeable in the early years of the TTDF's existence but were gradually resolved as more and more trained officers and NCOs were able to assume responsibilities.

Training for the TTDF was largely done locally for other ranks but officers of the TTR were trained for one year at the RMA Sandhurst while officers for the TTCG were trained at the BRNC Dartmouth. There were also extensive training courses conducted in or by the United States and while there were some lacunae in operational training, overall the standard of basic training and the quality of personnel was quite high and professionalism carefully inculcated in the officer corps and other ranks.

Messerschmitt-Bölkow-Böhm MBB Bo.105 CBS-4 – used for police support by NHSL before its loss. (Photo by Author)

The TTR in particular has always had a somewhat problematic conceptual role in the defence structure of the country. While the TTCG had a very clear maritime responsibility and embarked upon an equipment acquisition process that was well suited to its intended role and function, emerging as a very capable maritime unit with an enviable regional reputation, the TTR had no clear role. The TTPS still clung to its paramilitary trappings and in the absence of internal unrest beyond the ability of the police to handle, there was little call upon the TTR in respect of aggressive internal security duties. However, the TTR's training focused heavily on internal security with industrial unrest looming as a potential challenge in the late 1960s and early 1970s with training in crowd dispersal and control of industrial facilities being emphasised at some length with exercises including the occupation of such facilities against strikers.

One aspect that was heartening was the fact that the officer corps of the TTDF took its responsibilities as being loyal to the constitution very seriously. Despite a mutiny in 1970, occasioned in large part, as detailed below, by conditions within the regiment, the TTDF viewed itself as apolitical.

The TTDF, prior to 1990, saw no combat but in 1970, during political upheavals associated with the Black Power Revolution, elements of the TTR mutinied, led by Lieutenants Raffique Shah and Rex LaSalle. This mutiny while politically alarming, lacked any clear objective and ended in a tame surrender by the mutineers and later their acquittal by a court martial. The TTCG, in contrast, remained completely loyal during 1970 and some tension between the formation has existed ever since.

The 1970 Mutiny

The bizarre events of 1970 have been given all manner of political spin by people who were participants in the event and some officers either currently serving or now retired from the TTDF. Several intelligence reports on the 1970 mutiny indicated that there was political involvement in the events at Teteron Barracks, set against a tense political environment where the TTDF found itself witnessing a debate between a revivalist Afro-Trinidadian identity and a military still rooted in a colonial past.

Roots of Discontent

Lieutenant Colonel Joffre Serrette had taken over command in 1964. His subordinates were a motley crew of former civil servants, teachers and associated personnel with minimal military training and even less command experience. There were exceptions to this rule but many junior officers saw their seniors as uniformed popinjays with more interest in the cut of their uniforms and their perks.

In contrast, a new generation of officers, trained at Sandhurst and Mons were trying to turn the TTR into some sort of fighting force, though this might have been an exaggeration since resource and manpower constraints meant that at best the TTR could develop relatively limited combat capabilities. It was and is incapable of defending the country against a major external invasion as the correlation of forces and capabilities will always be against the TTDF.

There is, however, little doubt that with the arrival of these new officers, with a new outlook and new training, there was an increasing emphasis on training and readiness levels improved. The induction of a new generation of small arms and support equipment – the 7.62mm SLR, the first batch of which was received from Australia in 1966, replaced the .303 Rifle No.4 and the FN MAG GPMG replaced the Bren and Vickers guns, while the Carl Gustav recoilless rifle made its debut along with the 81mm mortar platoon and two Dingo armoured scout cars – helped solidify the feeling that the TTR was capable of being more than a mere ceremonial force and adjunct to the police service and was emerging, in its own right, as a viable entity.

There have been many theories, some ascribing political motives, as to the cause of the 1970 mutiny of the TTR. There is little doubt that the TTR was deeply concerned about the growing political and social unrest that characterised the street protests of 1970. It was also concerned about the increasing industrial and labour unrest supporting the Black Power movement and was inevitably concerned as to its role, should it have been called upon to aid the police in suppressing any protests. There was also the difference between the older officers, largely opposing the street protests, and the younger, radical idealists.

Yet another factor, however, was the lackadaisical approach to disciplinary matters within the TTR itself. This manifested itself in an inability of the senior ranks to deal even with insubordination on the part of junior officers towards seniors and a reluctance to enforce discipline. Major Hylton-Edwards recorded an instance of 2nd Lieutenant Lasalle raising his voice to the then CO TTR, Stanley Johnson, following a rowdy dinner in the Officers' Mess when five junior officers – led apparently by Lasalle and Shah – began banging cutlery and singing 'We Shall Overcome'. This lack of discipline stemmed from a leadership dispute.[18]

The real reason for tension in the TTR was directly related to a loss in confidence in the senior leadership. In 1968, Serrette had been arbitrarily relieved of his command by the government following rumours of a rift with the then Minister of Home Affairs, Gerard Montano, and replaced by Stanley Johnson, who was suddenly promoted to full Colonel in a remarkably short time.[19] This was not a popular decision among other officers and Stanley Johnson himself seems to have commanded little respect neither in regard to his ability nor his personality. In contrast, junior officers such as 2nd Lieutenants Raffique Shah and Rex LaSalle were quite charismatic and forceful leaders who also were politically aware of the developments going on in the country around them.

Other issues of a more prosaic nature, such as salaries (ordinary private soldiers then received between TT$ 24 and TT$ 36 a week, while lieutenants earned TT$ 336 a month) were major points of contention, though it has to be said, no arm of the government sector was particularly well paid at the time.[20]

Colonel Johnson came under severe criticism for being unable to address key issues in the TTR, namely a continuing shortage of manpower and deteriorating living conditions at the various barracks. The state of the regiment's fleet of vehicles was abysmal (something that would recur in 1990) and the combat effectiveness of the TTR was very debatable. Shah and LaSalle asserted that they tried to bring this to the attention of their superiors but this was to no avail. It was reported that on the eve of the revolt nearly one in six of the 600 personnel in the TTR were on sick-leave with some being deemed psychiatric cases.[21] This was a shocking level for a small force.

The Revolt

The TTR revolt was sparked in part at least by the decision of Prime Minister Williams to declare a State of Emergency on 21 April 1970. Led by Shah and LaSalle, some 150 soldiers mostly young – between the ages of 19 and 30 – were involved in the mutiny.[22] The takeover of the Teteron army barracks and the seizure of the ammunition bunker was conducted without any loss of life, with the only casualty being Major Henry Christopher who was wounded in his hand trying to wrestle a rifle way from Shah.

One of the two TTCG vessels – TTS *Trinity* – fired on the bunker with its 40mm Bofors gun from a range of 300m. This was remarkably close as the rebel soldiers had by this time armed themselves with rifles and GPMGs and had secured the six Carl Gustav 84mm rocket launchers held by the TTR. The Bofors fire was completely ineffective but it did give rise to a popular myth of their action having saved the day for Trinidad. Reality was somewhat more prosaic and less dramatic and the mutineers' failure to return fire saved the *Trinity*.[23]

The rebelling soldiers had amassed a substantial arsenal which included six Carl Gustav recoilless rifles, over 500 SLRs, several hundred submachine guns, 20 GPMGs, hundreds of Mills 36 grenades and well over 250,000 rounds of ammunition. In addition, they secured the five 81mm mortars of the mortar platoon.[24] There was no unit with this level of firepower available to stop the rebelling soldiers, the TTCG included.

In the capital Port of Spain, the Trinidad and Tobago Police Service (TTPS) was hastily armed with a bewildering array of small arms but mainly .303 Rifle No.4s and submachine guns. A few soldiers, many of whom were recent recruits and fresh out of training, were issued with SLRs and five rounds each as the country braced for a possible move by the mutineers from Teteron into the capital. The resistance that the TTPS and soldiers could mount was very limited at best and it is perhaps fortunate that it was not tested in any way with no lives lost.

The TTCG remained the most loyal military force available to the government with its 150 men and two patrol boats – TTS *Trinity* and TTS *Courland Bay* – being armed with 40mm Bofors. Its sole aircraft a Cessna 337 (9YA) piloted by Lieutenant Archibald overflew the rebel positions and tried to keep the government apprised of military movements and activity in the affected areas. Once again, the mutineers demonstrated remarkable restraint – perhaps indicative of their unclear motives – in that they did not fire on the aircraft, which, being unarmed, slow and low-flying, was vulnerable to ground fire from the mutineers' weapons.[25]

The TTCG, however, did arm its personnel with the infantry weapons it had available; SLRs and submachine guns were issued and landings practised from launches. With their additional armament of ship and land-based machine guns plus the undoubtedly effective 40mm Bofors L-60s aboard TTS *Trinidad* and TTS *Courland Bay*, the TTCG was the only military force that remained "loyal" to the government and, despite being very vulnerable to the mutineers' weapons, was prepared to confront and, if necessary, fire upon the mutineers.

A column of anywhere between 150 and 200 soldiers, armed with submachine guns, rifles, GPMGs and Carl Gustavs along with primed hand grenades was readied to move into Port of Spain. TTS *Trinity* chose once again to engage at a range of some 600m, well within the effective range of the Carl Gustavs' HE rounds.

The *Courland Bay* was still at TTCG HQ at Staubles Bay and had taken on board all shore personnel in case the facility needed to be evacuated. Some reports suggest that the *Trinity* was targeted by the weapons of the mutineers but they did not fire on the vessel though both sides knew the ship's clear vulnerability.[26]

In the course of the Trinity's shelling, one soldier, Private Clyde Bailey was wounded and had to be evacuated. Despite strong feelings that action should be taken, Shah and LaSalle, after abortive attempts to contact both the Trinity and the Cessna 337 9YA, and in spite of their overwhelming firepower, decided to withdraw back to Teteron to await developments.[27] In this sense, the lack of a clear agenda on the part of the mutineers was abundantly evident and as such whatever plans they may have had for moving into Port of Spain were not supported by any discernible political plans. The withdrawal to Teteron also saw the first steps towards de-escalation with Lieutenant Commander Mervyn Williams of the TTCG being sent as an intermediary given that he was widely respected and viewed very much as a paternal figure in both the TTR and the TTCG.[28]

The government of Prime Minister Eric Williams had been very reluctant to call for any external intervention during this crisis. However, he realised that his hastily and patchily armed police forces and few loyal soldiers could not resist a concerted push by the mutineers into Port of Spain, and given the reach of the Carl Gustavs and their undoubted efficacy against the TTCG's patrol boats, there must have been real concerns as to whether the Williams government could survive this crisis, though it is by no means certain that the toppling of the government was on the mutineers' political agenda.

During this confrontation, it was reported that a Venezuelan task force including at least two frigates had sortied towards Trinidad.[29] The vessels were intercepted by the TTCG and requested to return, which they did.

Despite holding Teteron for ten days, Shah and his colleagues agreed to talks and after Colonel Serrette was re-installed as CO – now promoted to Brigadier – issues such as the release of all political detainees and an amnesty for all participants in the mutiny were discussed. The mutineers gradually disarmed, initially by removing the firing pins from their heavy weapons – the Carl Gustavs in particular. Ninety men were charged with treason and mutiny, of whom 40 would be court-martialled. Several, including Shah and LaSalle, were sentenced to prison but, on appeal, the sentences were quashed and they were freed in 1972.[30]

Following the events of 1970, the TTR made strenuous efforts to reinvent and rehabilitate itself although it had to suffer the indignity of having its Carl Gustavs impounded by the police or sent to the Coast Guard for a number of years. The police service was emboldened by the temporary loss of face on the part of the TTR and sought to strengthen its paramilitary nature which it was able to do through the induction of many of the same small arms used by the TTDF and also by strengthening its Guard and Emergency Branch of heavily armed police officers.

The TTCG also played a role in rehabilitating the TTR with a deliberate effort to include parties of soldiers aboard naval vessels to enable them to participate in routine boarding operations as well as to introduce them to the maritime environment, and to build bonds between the formations which had been severely strained by the mutiny and the TTCG's role in attempting to suppress it. That being said, there was little animosity at most levels since a new generation of officers had replaced those tainted during the TTR mutiny and had moved on with improving the regiment's capabilities. These were to play a major role in the events of 1990.

Trinidad and Tobago's Day of Infamy[31]

Between the evening of 27 July 1990 and the afternoon of 1 August 1990, the Republic of Trinidad and Tobago suffered and overcame the second major challenge to its tradition of constitutional democracy since its independence from the United Kingdom in 1962. The citizens of the country witnessed the spectacle of the imposing figure of Imam Yasin Abu Bakr announcing the 'overthrow' of the government of Prime Minister Arthur N.R. Robinson.

While the death toll of 24 was relatively modest, it was a colossal shock to Trinidad's national psyche. The property damage and the consequent damage to the economy was severe and the country took a considerable period of time to achieve any degree of normality. However, the effects of the insurrection were not so much physical but rather the unleashing of hitherto underestimated ideologies of violent Islam. This was to have a major impact some 25 years later when the extent of Trinidadian involvement in ISIS became known.

The Trinidad and Tobago Regiment up to 1990

In 1990, the TTR was a small service, with two battalions constituting its entire strength. One of these battalions was a dedicated infantry formation while the other was designated the service support battalion and was responsible for all logistics and support elements including, it appears, a single mortar platoon of five 81mm mortars which, alongside some company level 60mm mortars, constituted the entire indirect fire support element of the TTR. The TTR also had a small force of Shorland armoured vehicles including at least three armoured cars and two armoured personnel carriers.[32] These vehicles, acquired in the 1980s, replaced the two Dingo armoured cars and were armed with smoke grenade dispensers and the armoured cars were frequently deployed with turret mounted GPMGs with the vehicle commander often carrying a B-300 rocket launcher as these became available in the mid to late 1980s. These vehicles were used for convoy escort and were deployed during the TTR's exercises in the 1980s.

The TTR was, in 1990, largely but not completely, re-equipped with Israeli Galil 5.56mm assault rifles which replaced the earlier L1A1 SLRs of British origin. The 7.62mm FN MAG GPMG was the standard automatic weapon for fire support, supplemented by a number of M60s from the United States and a small number of M2HB .5-inch heavy machine guns. Sterling and Uzi submachine guns were also in widespread use and were widely employed by radio operators with the latter being a particular favourite among the TTR's Special Forces. The re-equipment with 5.56mm weapons was far from complete in 1990 with perhaps only one-half of all personnel being re-equipped with Galils and with an average of only two Galils being available for every three infantrymen. The shortfall was made up by stocks of the old, reliable SLR which remained a very visible weapon among soldiers outside of the 1st Infantry Battalion and perhaps was even found among this formation.

It should be noted that the TTCG was still largely armed with the SLR and Sterling submachine gun but possessed two L-70 Bofors guns aboard CG-5 and CG-6 along with a 20mm weapon aboard CG-4 plus a plethora of heavy and medium machine guns aboard ship, making their deployable firepower not inconsiderable.[33]

Additionally, a number of Carl Gustav 84mm recoilless rifle systems remained ostensibly in service, having been purchased prior to 1970. These had been largely supplanted by Israeli B-300 systems – at least 13 of which were in service. The procurement of the B-300, as in the case of the Carl Gustav, was somewhat puzzling since the TTR did not envisage any encounter with a hostile force equipped with any type of armour. While the high-explosive rounds of the Carl Gustav were useful in demolishing buildings or hostile strongpoints, given that the TTR had not been trained to any extent in urban combat, the procurement of these weapons is one of the more curious acquisitions made by the TTR. However, during the 1990 insurrection, the B-300s were to come into their own with devastating effects both physical and psychological.

The 1st Infantry Battalion – led by Lieutenant Colonel Hugh Vidal – fielded some five rifle companies, designated 'A' to 'E, while the service support battalion – led by Lieutenant Colonel Carlton Alfonso – had two companies, an administrative company and a support company. The TTR had a total strength in 1990 of 1,513 personnel – 49 officers and 1,464 personnel below officer rank. For its modest size, the TTR was adequately equipped. A reserve force of approximately three rifle companies was available through the Volunteer Defence Force. The force was a well-balanced unit and possessed adequate firepower for its single infantry battalion.

The Trinidad and Tobago Coast Guard up to 1990

The TTCG began its operational history with two 103ft Vosper Ltd patrol boats –TTS *Trinity* (CG-1) and TTS *Courland Bay* (CG-2) – commissioned on 20 February 1965, each 31.4m long, displacing 123 tonnes and armed with L60 40mm guns. These were followed by TTS *Chaguaramas* (CG-3) and TTS *Buccoo Reef* (CG-4), commissioned on 18 March 1972, each 31.5m long and displacing 125 tonnes, being armed with Oerlikon 20mm guns. CG-1 and CG-2 were decommissioned in 1986 and CG-3 and CG-4 in 1992.[34]

These Vospers were followed on 15 June 1980 by two modified Spica-class vessels – TTS *Barracuda* (CG-5) and TTS *Cascadura* (CG-6) – each 40.6m long and displacing 210 tonnes. These vessels were equipped with L70 40mm guns plus Oerlikon 20mm weapons. These vessels were very advanced for their time and were well-liked locally.

Following a failed attempt at local repair and refurbishment in the late 1990s, these vessels were removed from service after nearly 15 years of inactivity. CG-5 was scrapped. While CG-6 remained ostensibly on the fleet list in 2019, at Chaguaramas Heliport, it was completely derelict, bereft of sensors, engines, weapons and accommodation. In 1990 both CG-5 and CG-6 were suffering from spares shortages and in dire need of overhaul.[35] These overhauls never took place and the vessels never achieved their full operational status, with their subsequent withdrawal from operational service and undignified fate epitomising the lack of foresight post-1990. This was demonstrated in the failure to overhaul and refurbish assets which served the country extremely well and which had been purchased as part of a well thought out fleet expansion programme that stretched from 1965 to 1980.

On 27 August 1982, four Souter Wasp 17m-class (TTS *Plymouth* CG27, TTS *Caroni* CG28, TTS *Galeota* CG29, and TTS *Moruga* CG30) were commissioned. In addition, the Coast Guard was augmented in the mid to late 1980s with vessels from the disbanded Police Marine Branch – one Sword-class patrol craft (TTS *Matelot* CG 33) and two Wasp 20m-class (TTS *Kairi* CG31 and TTS *Moriah* CG 32). All of these vessels have now been decommissioned.[36]

The years 1986 to 1995 saw the decommissioning of almost all of the TTCG patrol assets and the de facto retirement of CG-5 and CG-6 for want of serviceability as well as the inability of the TTCG to undertake routine maintenance due to severe funding shortfalls. This left the formation incapable of performing its assigned tasks on any sort of credible basis. This period, not surprisingly, saw a significant increase in narcotics and illegal weapons being shipped through Trinidadian waters.

On 10 June 1989, all vessels belonging to the Police Marine Branch, the immigrations, prisons, fire services and the port authority, were handed over to the TTCG to be made operational. When the vessels were handed over, not one of the eight launches of the Police Marine Branch was operational. Within six weeks, all eight launches were restored to service and put into a patrol cycle.[37] This spoke highly of the ethos of the TTCG which was attempting to continue its work despite severe resource shortfalls. The induction of these vessels provided the TTCG with assets for routine patrols at a time when its resources were under severe strain for want of repairs and spare parts due to budgetary issues.

In 1990, the Trinidad and Tobago Coast Guard was in dire straits with vessels being short of spares, in need of dry docking, and crew training suffering for want of seagoing experience. While CG-3, CG-4, CG-5 and CG-6 were nominally in commission, evidence suggests that only CG-6 was fully operational at the time of the 1990 insurrection. CG-5 was down to one engine while the hull of CG-4 was in such poor shape restricting it to calm waters. Despite these shortcomings, the force of CG-4, CG-5 and CG-6 was still the most potent naval unit in the English-speaking Caribbean and was worthy of some respect.

CG-3 was in commission but not operational to any extent. These three vessels did sortie during the insurrection with hastily gathered crews and were supported by a motley mix of support vessels including some of the Souter Wasp boats named above. Personnel strength was approximately 550 inclusive of its small Air Wing and its commando unit, the Special Naval Unit (SNU).

Air Assets up to 1990

The TTDF has had a military aviation component since 1966 when the Air Wing of The Trinidad and Tobago Coast Guard was formed with a single Cessna 337 (serial TTDF-1) which served from 1966 to 1972 when it was replaced with a Cessna 402 Utiliner (serial 201).[38]

A brief flirtation with military helicopters began with the formation of the Rotary Wing Flight in 1973 with the first of four Aerospatiale SA-341 G/H Gazelles (serials 9Y-TFN, 9Y-TFO and 9Y-TGU) coming into service. However, by 1976, these were transferred to the Air Division of the Ministry of National Security which morphed into the National Helicopter Services Limited in 1990.[39] This entity performed helicopter operations in support of the Ministry of National Security but also performed civilian tasks and earned revenue by supporting the country's offshore oil installations. It was and remains a civilian entity with neither its pilots nor ground-crew being military or police personnel.

In service, the Gazelles were joined by Sikorsky S-76 helicopters from 1981 with three such helicopters being eventually delivered (9Y-TGW, 9Y-TGX and 9Y-TJW).[40] The S-76 in its various incarnations was to prove very popular in Trinidadian service and the type is still in service. It should be noted that although the NHSL helicopters were deployed in support of the TTDF during the insurrection of 1990, they remained painted in their highly visible civilian colours of orange and white which, while not as garish as their current bright red and black livery, rendered their aircraft somewhat conspicuous to anyone looking at them. The country lacked any dedicated military helicopter force and did not yet have an effective law enforcement air support doctrine.

Besides the addition of a single Cessna 310 in 1985 (serial 202), the Air Wing of the Coast Guard stagnated for decades with capabilities being severely limited and aircraft being procured second-hand rather than new. The acquisition of an old Cessna 172 in 1991 added little to the Air Wing's capabilities and it was withdrawn from service

Cessna 310 of the Trinidad and Tobago Coast Guard Air Wing. (Photo by Author)

Cessna 402 and Cessna 310 of the Trinidad and Tobago Coast Guard Air Wing. (Photo by Author)

Cessna 172 and C-26 of the Trinidad and Tobago Coast Guard Air Wing. (Photo by Author)

in 1994 but spent at least six years occupying space in the Air Wing's sole hangar propped on tyres. The Cessna 402 was withdrawn from service in 1998 but again remained in the hangar on supports for at least two years.

In 1990, therefore, the air assets available to the TTDF included two Cessnas – a 310 and a 402 – and the four helicopters of the NHSL. These assets were not extensively deployed largely because of a lack of need but the helicopters did fly several sorties in support of the TTR. The NHSL helicopters, in particular its S-76 fleet, were placed at the disposal of the TTDF's Special Forces contingents.

1990 – A Baptism of Fire

The Jamaat-al-Muslimeen mustered a fighting strength of some 114 men. These were led by Imam Yasin Abu Bakr, with Bilal Abdullah acting as his effective second in command. Both Bakr and Abdullah along with a few others had received varying levels of training in weapons handling and terrorist tactics in Libya with some emphasis being placed on the construction of car bombs and other improvised explosive devices.[41] The majority of their 'troops' were semi-trained youth with a smattering of older personnel and were largely of Afro-Trinidadian descent from urban areas in Trinidad. They were motivated but lacked a clear objective.

The origin of the Jamaat's weapons is most curious as, with their alleged Libyan connections, one might have expected at least some Soviet-bloc weapons to enter their arsenal. Rather, the Jamaat relied on an elaborate and highly effective smuggling network with purchases being made legitimately in the United States and then smuggled into Trinidad sandwiched between sheets of plywood. These were then cleared through customs thanks to Muslimeen supporters in the customs and excise division – one of whom was very well placed to deliver such services.[42] This network was outstandingly successful in allowing the Jamaat to build a large weapons stockpile.

Weapons available to the insurrectionists were almost exclusively civilian pattern semi-automatic weapons available commercially in the United States. There was a preponderance of Ruger Mini 14s and a few M1 carbines were noticed along with a number of pump action shotguns. There was a mix of handguns, both semi-automatic pistols and revolvers, and a number of grenades were captured when the final surrender took place. There were no support weapons of any kind and there was no evidence of the insurrections having been trained to the extent necessary to make effective use of their weapons in urban or open combat.

TTR soldiers on patrol in Port of Spain during the 1990 Muslimeen Insurrection. (Trinidad Express Newspapers)

In the aftermath of the insurrection an assessment of the arsenal available to the Jamaat conducted by US Special Agents Thomas J. Bailey and Adam R. Price revealed that of the 135 weapons used in the insurrection and which were subsequently surrendered, 105 were purchased by Jamaat agent Louis Haneef, a resident of Florida. These included 17 Mossberg 'Persuader' and 26 Winchester 12-gauge shotguns, 25 M1 Carbines plus several dozen Ruger Mini-14 rifles.[43] The use of commercial pattern weapons is particularly noteworthy as is the manner of acquisition.

The Muslimeen Strikes

The first target of the Jamaat-al-Muslimeen was on the headquarters of the TTPS located on Sackville Street, Port of Spain. At approximately 5:57 p.m. on Friday 27 July 1990, a young man of African descent was observed approaching the Sackville Street entrance of the TTPS HQ[44]. A police officer, Special Reserve Police Constable Solomon McLeod approached the young man and they engaged in a brief discussion, pointing to the nearby Sacred Heart Church. As the young man walked away, he fired eight rounds into SRP McLeod, plus one into the air.

The death of SRP McLeod, and the shot into the air, was the signal for the occupants of a green station wagon to drive the vehicle from around the corner of St Vincent Street, whereupon, four occupants alighted, and the vehicle was then driven over the corpse of SRP McLeod and into TTPS HQ whereupon it exploded.

While this was happening, an assault group of 36 Jamaat members moved towards the Parliament building, fully armed and meeting no resistance from any policemen on patrol. The Trinidad and Tobago Fire Service, which emerged as unheralded heroes of the insurrection, responded immediately to the blaze at TTPS HQ but were forced to withdraw after coming under heavy gunfire from the Jamaat, though no casualties were apparently incurred.[45] The proximity of TTPS HQ, the main Port of Spain Fire Station and the Red House Parliament building are particularly noteworthy. The distances allowed for the easy movement of the Jamaat insurrectionists.

Storming the Red House

The attack on the Red House, the seat of parliament, was the centrepiece of the Jamaat-al-Muslimeen's assault. It was a brilliantly conceived operation that succeeded by any metric. At about 5:45 p.m., Hon. Joseph Toney, a minister in the Prime Minister's office, was on his feet addressing the chamber and engaging in some of the usual crosstalk that engaged the Trinidad and Tobago Parliament, this time with Mr Trevor Sudama, of the newly formed United National Congress (UNC) and once Mr Toney's cabinet colleague. Mr Toney asked him 'Who is your leader?' At that point there was a lot of noise and gunshots and the chamber was stormed by an assault group of 36 Jamaat insurrectionists led by Bilal Abdullah, a close lieutenant of Imam Abu Bakr and one who was subsequently seen as the Jamaat's most capable leader during the insurrection.[46]

Initially, given their uniform-like garb, Mr Toney thought 'it was a military takeover'; however, since the gunmen were chanting 'Allahu Akbar', the members of parliament soon realised that the gunmen were Muslims, with the gradual realisation that they were members of the Jamaat-al-Muslimeen who singled out government ministers and overwhelmed the security detail.[47]

TTR personnel armed with SLRs using a civilian pick-upi in 1990. (Trinidad Express)

weapons being sent separately and housed in a vehicle near to Radio Trinidad, on Maraval Road. The assault began after 6:00 p.m. and resulted in a complete takeover of Radio Trinidad within a few minutes. Shabaaz announced that his intentions were not to harm any of the staff members of Radio Trinidad and indicated that if they cooperated all would be well. The assault group met no resistance of any kind as there was no security presence.[49] Emmett Hennessy, a radio host, escaped but was shot and injured. An employee, Pius Mason, was shot and severely injured apparently in error. This infuriated Bakr who was quite enraged when he heard of the incident and he took measures to ensure that the civilian employees at Radio Trinidad and TTT were protected over the subsequent days as the army tightened its cordon and contained the insurgents.

Several civilians were shot. At least two – Mervyn Teague and Lorraine Caballero – being killed as they tried to escape or panicked. Ms Caballero's death was particularly traumatic as she was shot in the stomach and left to bleed to death. In addition, one member of parliament, Leo Des Vignes was shot, perhaps because of his panicking during the invasion of the parliament chamber. He later died of his wounds. At the parliament building, the following deaths in various circumstances are known to have occurred:

ASP Roger George
Estate Constable Malcolm Basanta
George Francis
Arthur Guiseppi
Helen Lavia
Lorraine Caballero
Mervyn Teague[48]

Attack 3: Seizing Radio Trinidad and Trinidad and Tobago Television

The assault on Radio Trinidad was led by Jamal Shabaaz who indicated that his group of 12 men left Mucurapo in three cars with

TTR B-300 operator in position during the insurrection of 1990. (Trinidad Express)

Attack on TTT

While Imam Yasin Abu Bakr was ostensibly in charge of the assault on TTT, the actual operation was led by one Kala Akii-Bua. Entry into TTT was as simple and as facile as that of Radio Trinidad with no resistance being encountered. Once again, the assault force assembled in multiple vehicles and collected their weapons near to their target site. Once again, despite ostensible TTPS Special Branch surveillance, the Jamaat was able to assemble unimpeded.

Within TTT, senior journalist Jones P. Madiera was confronted by the sight of gunmen in the building and, along with veteran journalist Raoul Pantin, was made to lie on the floor while the other employees of TTT were assembled by the assault group. Initially, there was speculation that it was an armed robbery until the arrival of Imam Abu Bakr. All women and children were allowed to leave along with two German technicians present on a training course. However, 26 hostages were held by the Jamaat-al-Muslimeen at TTT.[50]

Following the capture of the country's sole television station, the stage was set. It was at about 6:20 p.m. that the Imam Abu Bakr made his now famous (or infamous) broadcast:

> Good evening, ladies and gentlemen. We would like to take this opportunity to inform you that at about 6.00 p.m. this afternoon the Government of Trinidad and Tobago has been overthrown. The Prime Minister and members of the Cabinet are at present under arrest. The military are in contact with us and we are asking everybody to lay down their arms so that there can be a peaceful transition. We're asking people not to involve in looting or any form of unlawful actions or else they will have to pay the consequences thereof. We would like to keep you informed with a further news broadcast as we proceed.[51]

The TTDF Reacts

The TTDF was, like all agencies, caught unawares but reacted quite quickly within its limited resources and its lack of prior experience in these matters. In this regard, the football match referred to earlier, offered the regiment quite a bit of assistance. The CO TTR, Colonel Ralph Brown, was at the said match when at 6:00 p.m., minutes after the attack began, he was informed by one Felix Hernandez and, after gathering all members of the TTR and TTDF who had gathered there, left immediately for the TTR's small base, Camp Ogden, located in St James, near Port of Spain.[52]

Colonel Brown recalled that one of the first things he did on hearing of this was to request all members of the TTR to leave the stadium and assemble, making the announcement over the stadium's public address system.[53] Nearly 200 TTR soldiers had been issued passes to the football game and were available at short notice.[54]

By 6:15 p.m., Captain Rodney Smart had 'closed the gates' and confined the personnel at both Camp Ogden and the TTR's forward base for anti-marijuana operations at Camp Cumuto. In terms of available forces, the TTR had one sub-strength rifle company deployed at Camp Cumuto, 60 personnel from both the TTR and TTCG were gathered from the football match and despatched to Camp Ogden, plus whatever personnel were in camp at the time. Available forces were aided by the recent induction of four hundred privates into the TTR over a period of 12 months.[55]

While CO 1st Battalion TTR, Lieutenant Colonel Hugh Vidal, despatched two officers to ascertain what was happening, Colonel Joseph Theodore, the Chief of Defence Staff, having also been apprised of the situation, despatched two warrant officers for a similar fact-finding mission. At this point, neither Colonels Brown nor Theodore or any of their subordinates had an inkling of a hostage situation being evident with only the bombing of the TTPS HQ and gunfire being then known.[56]

At about 7:00 p.m. Colonel Brown was able to return from his football game to the forward TTR post at Camp Ogden and there he met Colonel Theodore and Lieutenant Colonel Vidal. At this point they waited for the nightly television news at 7:00 p.m., which is something of an institution in Trinidad, more so in 1990, but it was only at about 7:15 p.m. that they saw Imam Abu Bakr appear on television with the dawning realisation that the TTT studios had been seized by the Jamaat. Colonel Brown at 7:30 p.m. gave Major Joseph orders to secure the Nelson Exchange of the Trinidad and Tobago telephone company to ensure no misuse of the communications network.[57]

Within its resources, the TTR moved as quickly as possible to contain the Jamaat within a limited geographic area and had done so with forces at its disposal, which were, admittedly very limited. Camp Ogden was to prove a rallying point for military personnel but was neither stocked nor provisioned to properly outfit such forces and the fact that Major Joseph could only assemble the equivalent of a rifle platoon a full hour after Camp Ogden was closed and personnel confined, illustrates problems faced in generating combat units.

Of equal importance, however, is the poor level of communications and coordination between the individual battalions and sometimes individual officers. Fortunately, this did not have a major impact owing to the overall incompetence of the Jamaat and the fact that the insurrection was geographically contained quite quickly. This unfortunate state of affairs could have led to major problems as communications between the 1st Infantry Battalion and the 2nd Service and Support Battalion were particularly poor for the first 48 hours and the TTCG was not even informed until sometime later and was largely left to operate as it deemed fit.

The CO of the TTCG, Commander Kelshall, was not informed through official channels of the insurrection and was actually informed by his mother-in-law about the apparent attack on TTPS HQ and the subsequent address to the nation by Imam Abu Bakr.[58] He took care to secure the assets of the TTCG, perhaps fearful of an attack on the TTCG HQ at Staubles Bay or its subsidiary base at Harts Cut. This was by way of guaranteeing the security of the forces at his command. By way of specific tactical responses, the CO TTCG did the following:

secured the Coast Guard Station
instructed the Coast Guard vessels to carry out area patrols
set up road blocks
seized the heliport in Chaguaramas
established patrols
took over assets at Piarco airport where the Air Wing was based[59]

These responses were undoubtedly sound and well-reasoned. However, Commander Kelshall took the additional step of bringing his Special Naval Unit to a high state of alert and used it to bolster the security of his Coast Guard facilities, augmenting the armed ratings already deployed for that task.[60] Much effort was expended setting up machine gun nests and roadblocks around TTCG bases and moving ammunition on board TTCG vessels CG-4, CG-5 and CG-6.[61]

It was not until 7:30 p.m. that Colonel Brown spoke with him and, recognising the need for reinforcements, members of the Special Naval Unit were despatched to Port of Spain, with TTCG vehicles assisting in transporting ammunition to the TTR.[62]

Later, at the request of Colonel Theodore, Commander Kelshall deployed CG-4 (TTS *Buccoo Reef*), CG-5 (TTS *Barracuda*) and CG-6 (TTS *Cascadura*) to protect Port of Spain harbour and the Coast Guard bases at Hart's Cut and Staubles Bay.[63]

The TTCG's control of the Air Wing came to the fore when on Saturday morning, Lieutenant Commander Curtis Roach, Lieutenant Commander Bernard Baksh and retired Lieutenant Gaylord Kelshall came to Coast Guard Headquarters to offer their assistance. Lieutenant Kelshall, despite being long retired, was detailed to command the helicopters at the airport as he was the only military officer with aviation experience on hand. The civil helicopters of the National Helicopter Services Limited performed 46 military flights and were deployed to conduct reconnaissance and disperse looters.[64] In addition, the presence of the Coast Guard Air Wing, with its armed personnel at Piarco, enabled the airport to be secured relatively quickly once instructions were given, aided quite commendably by the airport's own security who acted to close the runway with efficiency.

The TTR found itself having to contain the Jamaat at the Red House, which was successfully done on the night of 27 July itself. Rather less successful, however, were attempts to contain and isolate the Jamaat at TTT and Radio Trinidad. This was largely due to a paucity of manpower and as will be noted was directly attributable to a failure of the TTPS to respond effectively to the situation and the inability of the Guard and Emergency Branch (GEB) of the TTPS to respond in any meaningful way to the insurrection or to effectively assist the TTR on that night. In fact, despite having a strength of several hundred personnel – armed and trained – the GEB was conspicuous by its absence on the first night of the insurrection and with the TTPS units in Port of Spain being largely unarmed, poorly trained and panicked after the destruction of their headquarters, the TTR found itself having to contend with the insurrection almost entirely on its own.

However, by the next day, reinforcements had arrived and the situation had largely stabilised as additional platoons from the TTR were able to secure perimeters around the TTT/ Radio Trinidad

TTR troops with SLRs using Trinidad and Tobago Electricity Commission vehicles. (Gayelle TV)

A Shorland armoured car and Shorland APC, as deployed in 1990. (Gayelle TV)

compounds and thus, in three locations, were able to completely isolate the Jamaat units from mutually supporting each other. This was a major factor in containing the military situation and it speaks to the amateurish nature of the insurrection and the limited resources of the TTPS, that a force of 114 insurgents was effectively contained by two platoons – about 60 men – of the TTR by the early hours of 28 July.

The military operations between 28 July and 1 August 1990 were quite anti-climactic in many ways as that early operation with 60 men effectively turned the insurrection into a combination of a siege and hostage situation. The operations also speak highly of the motivation and initiative taken by relatively junior officers in containing a force of unknown size.

Under orders, and in the early hours of 28 July, Captain George Clarke went with 22 men – a platoon minus – to an area west of the Queen's Park Savannah. This was done in order to secure a position around the Savannah and thereby dominate the area near to TTT. This unit was hastily put together and while they had rifles, basic kit and a load of ammunition, they did not necessarily have the weapons to which they were assigned. This force, however, was able to throw a cordon around TTT and establish and maintain a dominant presence in the area.[65]

Later that day, Saturday, 28th July, Major Joseph's troops came under heavy and sustained fire from the Jamaat forces in the Red House. As the TTR returned fire, an insurrectionist was shot trying to get into a vehicle outside the Red House. However, after Canon Knolly Clarke's intervention with the amnesty document described in the next chapter, at 6:00 p.m. Major Joseph was ordered to cease fire except if fired upon. However, members of the TTPS, once again displaying a lack of discipline, continued firing from the Cyril Duprey building apparently in defiance of orders from the Acting Commissioner of Police. A helicopter sortie established their presence and, after polite requests to get them to cease failed, Colonel Theodore threatened to have his special forces 'take them out'. At that point the TTPS ceased firing.[66]

Reinforcements from Alpha Company under the command of Major Ancil Antione arrived to reinforce Captain Clarke by noon on Saturday. Under fire, these forces made a multi-pronged attack against the Jamaat forces at TTT and were able to force the Jamaat into the TTT building and confine them there, thus totally containing the Jamaat at that location, injuring four insurrectionists in the process. Once again soon after 6:00 p.m., there was a ceasefire at TTT.[67]

With negotiations still going on, Major Joseph ordered a B-300 rocket to be launched against the Red House at an area away from the area of the parliamentary chamber where the hostages were held. This was done on Sunday morning when the Jamaat insurrectionists attempted a breakout from the Red House and engaged the TTR in a heavy gun battle. The B-300 caused a small fire that was easily extinguished by the Jamaat.[68]

The next day, on Monday afternoon, Captain Clarke's troops outside TTT directed heavy fire against the building and, even up to Tuesday, there were sporadic exchanges of gunfire between the TTR and the Jamaat. During this time, negotiations were continuing; the Prime Minister had been released and the release of all hostages was by then anticipated.[69]

However, on Wednesday, 1 August 1990 – the very day of release and surrender – Captain Clarke launched a B300 rocket against the TTT building. This was done ostensibly because Clarke wanted to 'test the capability of the building to withstand any attempt to penetrate it' and to remind the Jamaat that '... they were in a war'. Captain Clarke's actions, which had hitherto been exemplary was severely criticised for using the B-300 in such an apparently reckless manner.[70]

The insurrection left 24 people dead and 231 wounded, 133 of them in an orgy of looting and arson that followed leading to losses amounting to hundreds of millions of dollars.[71] Popular support for the insurrection was minimal but a total breakdown in law enforcement led to chaos, exploited by looters for personal gain. While the insurrection ended with the surrender of Bakr and his followers, they were acquitted of charges brought against them in the Trinidadian courts, which upheld an amnesty granted to them to secure the lives of the hostages. This has emboldened them and Bakr and his adherents have continued to occupy an important position of influence and prominence in the local Islamic community and the local criminal community.

The TTDF Today

Table 21: TTDF strength

	Total Strength	Army	Air Force	Coast Guard
Active personnel	4,657	2,680	420	1,557
Reserves	400 (full-time) and 224 (part-time)	400	80	144

The Trinidad and Tobago Regiment

The TTR has been the senior formation in the TTDF – despite its 1970 mutiny and slow rehabilitation thereafter – and has had a major share of personnel to date. The TTR is organised into four battalions – two infantry, one engineer, and one service and support. It currently lacks armour as its Shorland armoured cars and personnel carriers are now all derelict. Neither does it have any artillery beyond a single mortar platoon with 81mm mortars which were effectively non-operational until 2019 after being in storage for nearly 20 years for want of trained personnel.

The TTR is an infantry and support force with only soft-skinned vehicles for transport. The TTR lacks any ability to defend Trinidad's territorial integrity from foreign aggression and is not configured for a dedicated counter-insurgency function either. While the TTR has grown in size, its equipment has not kept pace with this expansion and with neither armour nor support weapons, the TTR is actually less well-equipped than it was in 1990 in some key respects. Israeli small arms – Galils and Negevs – dominate the inventory with the H&K MP5 and UMP being the principal submachine guns and 7.62mm GPMGs providing company and platoon level support.

In 2014–2015 there were some attempts to procure a force of APCs for the TTDF. In 2009, the requirement was set at a total of 19 APCs but no progress was made despite a number of wheeled internal security APCs being shortlisted for procurement. The entire proposal was shelved in 2016 and has not been resurrected. With no armour, no artillery and support weapons being limited to some company level 60mm mortars of questionable utility, a reactivated Support Weapons Detachment operating the 81mm mortars and a limited number of .50 Browning M2HB heavy machine guns alongside GPMGs of the M60 and FN MAG types, the TTDF is effectively a force of lightly armed infantry and is in dire need of an infusion of new equipment.

The TTCG – Recapitalised but Still Crippled

After a number of years with almost no serviceable vessels, the period 1999–2001 saw the TTCG receive a boost with the acquisition of the ex-Royal Navy Island-class OPV, HMS *Orkney* renamed TTS *Nelson* (CG-20) and four 82ft Point-class cutters, each displacing some 66 tonnes, from the United States (TTS *Corozal Point* CG7, TTS *Crown Point* CG8, TTS *Galera Point* CG9 and TTS *Bacolet Point CG10*). The Point-class cutters were nominally on strength until 2009–2010 when they were decommissioned but, in reality, they had been unseaworthy for some years prior. A half-hearted attempt was made to refit CG-7 but was abandoned It is a depressing fact that these vessels were well over 20 years old when procured. The stark reality was that not a single new-build patrol vessel was acquired between 1980 and 2009.[72]

In 2003–2004, the then government of Patrick Manning began a phased expansion of the formation which included the purchase of six new Austal PB30 Fast Patrol Craft (FPC) – CG11 TTS *Scarlet Ibis*, CG12 TTS *Hibiscus*, CG13 TTS *Humming Bird*, CG14 TTS *Chaconia*, CG 15 TTS *Poui* and CG16 TTS *Teak* – commissioned between 2009 and 2010, and two modified oil rig support vessels – each over 15 years old – armed and re-tasked as coastal patrol vessels (CPVs) – CG-21 TTS *Gaspar Grande* and CG-22 TTS

Point-class cutters GG-10 and CG-9. (TTCG)

Modified Spica-class vessel CG-6, TTS *Cascadura*. (TTCG)

CG-14, an Austal APB-30. (Austal)

CG-14 in 2013 – in very poor condition. (Photo by Author)

CG-6, TTS Cascadura. (TTCG)

Chacachare – commissioned on 23 April 2008. In addition, four Midnight Express Interceptors were delivered in 2005 and were extensively deployed in anti-narcotics operations.

The Austal APB 30s (CG-11 to CG-16) which were delivered between 2009 and 2010 experienced severe problems in Trinidadian service. The aluminium hulls of the vessels proved to be wholly inadequate for operations on the country's northern coast and severe problems were experienced with marine growth. Between 2010 and 2015, the Austal FPB 30s were the country's main maritime assets and they were tasked with roles for which they were not designed, placing undue stress on their somewhat delicate construction. Rather more puzzling were persistent electronic failures with radar and FLIR systems becoming unserviceable at an unusually high rate – only one of the two radars aboard usually being operational at any time.[73]

The 'crown jewels' of this expansion plan were three 90m-long OPVs – to be named the *Port of Spain, Scarborough* and *San Fernando* – ordered from VT Shipbuilding (later BAE Systems Surface Ships). Easily the most advanced vessels in the Caribbean (after the demise of the Cuban navy), the OPVs were adequately armed with 25mm and 30mm guns and possessed the ability to stage medium-lift helicopters from their flight decks. However, an overly ambitious integrated fire-control system and some unrealistic expectations from the TTCG in respect of the performance of the 30mm guns led to significant delays and problems during trials. In September 2010, the government of the then Prime Minister Kamla Persad-Bissessar cancelled the contract, a decision that in retrospect may have been ill-advised.

Of interest is the fact that the procurement of new vessels did not lead to a commensurate increase in the TTCG operational budget relative to the larger fleet. In addition, archaic bureaucratic procedures together with shortcomings in the TTCG engineering and maintenance branches combined to cripple efforts to restore serviceability to repairable vessels with contractors being unpaid for work done and vessels being laid-up for extended periods of time.

The Damen Acquisition – FCS 5009s and SPa 5009s

After deliberating and assessing the vessels and designs on offer, four CPVs were acquired from the Dutch shipyard, Damen, with two additional vessels of a similar design being acquired as 'utility vessels' but so armed and equipped that they could augment the four dedicated CPVs in the patrol role. The vessels selected were the SPa 5009 CPV and the FCS 5009 utility vessel. The CPVs were fitted with a surveillance system which drew heavily on high-end civilian products. In addition, they were fitted with a remotely controlled 20mm gun. The FCS 5009 was delivered in standard configuration but with accommodation increased for a larger crew, a manually operated 20mm gun (from TTCG stocks) and a slightly enhanced surveillance fit.

The two FCS 5009s were ordered as they were available for rapid delivery – sea trials taking place in December 2014. However, it was felt that the standard fit on the vessels was inadequate for the TTCG. In order to give the vessels more flexibility, the following modifications were made to the basic FCS 5009, aside from the necessary internal rearrangements to make them suitable for quasi-military use:

1) An adaptor for a GAM-B01 20mm gun was fitted forward. The wetness forward was not deemed an issue largely because any armed patrol duties were to be of a secondary nature to these vessels;

2) A Voyager II FLIR system was installed to provide a modicum of additional surveillance capability;

3) A Heila hydraulically operated knuckle-boom crane was installed which had the secondary function of being able to lower and recover a DI 1102 interceptor.[74]

The remains of CG-6. (Photo by Author)

CG-26, TTS *Quinam* of the Damen SPa 5009-class. (Photo by Author)

These two vessels – CG 23 TTS *Point Lisas* and CG 24 TTS *Brighton* – were delivered in the period May/June 2015 and duly commissioned into the TTCG.

The TTCG's SPa 5009s are easily the best equipped naval vessels in the English-speaking Caribbean. Unique among the ships of the region, they have a Combat Information Centre (CIC). The CIC housed displays – Transas NS4100s surveillance workstations – showing the radar, WECDIS and FLIR input with repeaters on the bridge. It was also envisaged that the CIC would house a dedicated secure communications suite supplied by Harris. Deliveries of the Harris equipment were delayed, leading to the vessels being commissioned without this equipment being fitted.[75]

The surveillance fit selected was a compromise using high quality civilian systems as opposed to dedicated military systems. The surveillance radar selected was the Kelvin Hughes X-Band Sharp Eye which emerged as the most cost-effective and available choice. The FLIR system chosen was the MU602CLW. A Saab R5 data link was also fitted along with a Rotheta RT-500M radio direction finder. It should be noted that the TTCG had expressed a desire for a Terma surveillance radar as fitted to the BAES OPVs. However, cost factors militated against this.

To enhance the interdiction capabilities of the SPa 5009, the standard stern-launched MST 750SR 7.5m RHIB was supplemented by a davit launched DI 1102 interceptor. While it was intended that the interceptor be launched and recovered while the mother vessel was moving, two incidents during familiarisation training may have led to a rethink in this regard.

The choice of weapon fell to the Rheinmetall/MSI Seahawk LW20A1 system. This proved to be a somewhat problematic choice as two rounds of firing trials – one in 2015 and one in 2016 – were aborted due to severe malfunctions. Even during those aborted trials, however, the accuracy of the system was excellent, but the aborted trials delayed the operationalisation of the vessels' weapons systems until late 2016.[76]

Owing to somewhat delayed payments, the four SPa 5009s were delivered between 2015 and 2016 and were designated and named as follows: CG 25 TTS *Speyside*, CG 26 TTS *Quinam*, CG 27 TTS *Moruga* and CG 28 TTS *Carli Bay*. Each of these vessels carried a DI 1102 interceptor, with two more being deployable on CG 23 and CG 24.

The LRPV procurement was not so fortunate as it was circumvented by the direct intervention of the then Prime Minister Persad-Bissessar who decided, against advice, to procure a ready-made, unarmed LRPV from CSSC of China which compared badly with the cancelled OPVs. The vessel procured, commissioned as CG-60, TTS *Nelson II*, was the largest military vessel in the English-speaking Caribbean but had very limited capabilities. Its surveillance system was not up to the standard.

By the end of 2016, from contracts signed under the People's Partnership government, the Coast Guard had:

One 79m Chinese-made LRPV
Four 50m Damen SPa 5009 CPVs
Two 50m Damen FCS 5009 armed utility vessels
Two 46m legacy CPVs returned to service.
Six legacy Austal APB 30 Fast Patrol Craft (of dubious serviceability)
Six DI 1102 onboard interceptors
Seventeen legacy interceptors (four of which were operational)
Six pirogues[77]

Serviceability problems have bedevilled the interceptor fleet but some efforts to restore unserviceable vessels have shown results but, even now, only six or eight of the 17 interceptors are operational. The 79m Chinese OPV has been largely inoperable since 2017.

However, the Damen patrol fleet has been experiencing a spate of maintenance problems, compounded by the temporary withdrawal of Dutch technicians due to the Wuhan Coronavirus pandemic. The

Table 22: The TTCG Fleet Today

Class	Manufacturer	Role	Original total	In service	Commissioned
Nelson II (ex-Haijian 1001)	Huangpu Shipyard	Offshore patrol vessel	1	1	2015
Cape-class	Austal	Offshore/Coastal Patrol Vessel	2	2	2021
Gaspar Grande	VT Shipbuilding	Coastal patrol vessel	2	2	2008
APB 30	Austal	Patrol craft	6	0	2009
Fast Crew Supplier 5009	Damen	Utility and Patrol Vessel	2	2	2015
Stan Patrol 5009	Damen	Coastal Patrol Vessel	4	4	2015
Interception Craft 1102	Damen	Interceptor craft	6	6*	2015
Bowen	n/k	Interceptor craft	2	0	1991
Midnight Express	Midnight Express	Interceptor craft	2	2 (unserviceable)	2005
Formula 111	n/k	Interceptor craft	2	2 (unserviceable)	2005
Phantom Enforcer Edgewater	Phantom	Interceptor craft Interceptor craft	3 2	3 (questionable serviceability) 2 (questionable serviceability)	n/k
Reform	n/k	Auxiliary vessel	1	0 (prison ship, unserviceable)	n/k

* Only six DI 1102 were purchased – four are mounted aboard the SPa 5009s and two can be carried aboard the FCS 5009s. There is reluctance to deploy the DI 1102s after a series of nearly fatal accidents.

expiration of the maintenance contract with Damen in 2021 may compound these problems. However, as of April 2021, all six Damen 50m vessels are operational.

The purchase of two Austal Cape-class patrol boats in 2018 will add to the existing fleet but it is unclear as to what role they would fulfil, being somewhat less capable than the SPa 5009 fleet in the CPV role but lacking the range to make them OPVs. These two Cape-class vessels are due to enter service in 2021 and the TTCG took delivery of CG 41 TTS *Port of Spain* and CG 42 TTS *Scarborough* on 14 May 2021.[78]

The first vessel – CG 41 – was launched by Austal on 3 December 2020, after a substantial delay occasioned by the Wuhan Coronavirus and its effect upon the operations of the shipyard. The contract was for AU$ 126 million, which would approximate to US$ 49 million per vessel with its attendant support package. These vessels mark the first export of the Cape-class, with the type having only been supplied to Australian agencies to date. Austal described the Trinidadian vessels in the following terms:

> The new TTCG *Capes* are based on the 58 metre aluminium monohull patrol boat, first developed by Austal in Australia for Australian Border Force. The vessels have a 4,000 nautical mile range and 28-day patrol cycle, with a crew of up to 22. Each *Cape* is equipped with two high-speed 7.3 metre rigid hull inflatable boats used for intercepting other vessels.[79]

In addition to its vessels, Trinidad and Tobago possesses an excellent coastal radar network with Elta El/M-2226 radars around the country's coast and also covers the islands of St Vincent and Grenada. While there have been occasional serviceability issues, these radars are functional and are being upgraded. This radar network has not prevented a thriving enterprise in smuggling illegal Venezuelan economic migrants, illegal weapons and narcotics from South America to Trinidad.

Air Arms – Growth and Decline

Trinidad and Tobago had no air force yet has one of the Commonwealth Caribbean's largest air arms comprising two separate entities – the Trinidad and Tobago Air Guard and the National Operations Centre Air Division. For a country with decidedly limited numbers of air assets, having two organisations has led to duplication of effort and a faulty procurement process that has ensured no compatibility of either aircraft or avionics.[80]

The Trinidad and Tobago Air Guard

The Trinidad and Tobago Air Guard (TTAG) as an independent service has had a very short life, being formed in 2005 by Cabinet Minute #1936 dated 28 July 2005 and inherited the force of the old TTCG Air Wing – two Piper Navajos, one Cessna 310, one Cessna 402 and two C-26s.[81]

The Cessna 402 was withdrawn from service in 1998 but again remained in the hangar on supports for at least two years. The late 1990s, however, were to bring a fresh lease of life to the outfit. At a time of enhanced counter-narcotics cooperation between the United States and Trinidad, the sight of US DEA Blackhawk helicopters was common at the Air Wing's base and in exchange, the United States transferred two seized PA-31 Piper Navajos (serials 203 and 204) and two Swearingen C-26A Metro aircraft (serials 215 and 216) to the Air Wing, thus infusing the stagnating outfit with new capabilities.

The Navajos, after becoming unserviceable (the bane of Trinidadian military equipment) were phased out in 2009–2010 but the C-26As form the most potent fixed wing assets of the force, renamed the Air Guard in 2005. C-26A serial 216 has been fitted with MR radar and FLIR while 215 appears to serve in the transport role capable of carrying 14 troops as far as Puerto Rico – a useful capability when handling disaster relief operations within the Caribbean.

Damen-built SPa 5009 TTS *Quinam* of the *Trinidad* and Tobago Coast Guard. (Damen Shipyards)

Two SPa 5009s of the TTCG – TTS *Moruga* and TTS *Carli Bay*, before departure to Trinidad. (Damen Shipyards)

TTS *Carli Bay* during trials. (Damen Shipyards)

Damen-manufactured FCS 5009 TTS *Brighton*, during trials. (Damen Shipyards)

A left-hand view of the C-26 light transport of the Trinidad and Tobago Coast Guard Air Wing. (Photo by Author)

a major serviceability problem that has only been partially alleviated through a somewhat uneasy partnership with the Canadian company, Provincial Aerospace Limited.[82]

The TTAG received its rotary wing assets in the form of four AW139s (9Y-AG311, 9Y-AG312, 9Y-AG313 and 9Y-AG314) helicopters which were delivered between 2011 and 2012. Costing over US$ 200 million, these four helicopters were plagued with a series of problems including structural cracks in their tail booms and required very delicate handling in air-conditioned hangars thus placing a heavy strain on the TTAG's limited infrastructure.

Exacerbating the problem was the fact that the TTAG had no trained helicopter pilots and was forced to employ foreign civilian pilots on contract while building flying hours for local pilots under some very generous contracts which worked to the detriment of the TTAG. The net result was that the helicopters remained severely restricted operationally, until their grounding in 2017.[83]

Almost completely neglected in the discourse on military aviation in Trinidad is the long-suffering C-26 fleet. The need for a replacement is acute as the aircraft are currently operating on borrowed time as spares and support for the type become ever more difficult to obtain. Furthermore, the maritime surveillance role performed by these aircraft is crucial to the country's border security and as these aircraft become progressively less serviceable, a huge gap will emerge in Trinidad's maritime domain awareness.

The fixed wing assets of the TTAG, therefore, were limited to three serviceable and notionally operational aircraft – two C-26As and one Cessna 310. Total flight time in 2008–2009 was over 250 hours in 121 missions – a figure substantially lower than the norm in 2000–2001 when over 350 hours were logged. This figure fell further by 2012 when the Cessna 310 was withdrawn from service without replacement. In addition, the C-26 aircraft began to show their age and equipment problems with the Elta M-2022 radar on board aircraft 216 seriously compromising the efficacy in the vital maritime surveillance role. Acute shortages of spares compounded

The National Operations Centre Air Division

Between 2010 and 2015, the NOC Air Division was a favoured outfit and received lavish budgetary attention perhaps in part because of its role in performing VIP transport missions for the then government of Prime Minister Kamla Persad-Bissessar. The NOC Air Division inherited assets from a defunct unit called the Special Anti-Crime Unit of Trinidad and Tobago (SAUTT), which operated at its zenith

Another look at the sole C-26 of the TTCG Air Wing. (Photo by Author)

four helicopters – one S-76A+, one AS.355 and two BO-105 CBS-4 – and a Westinghouse Skyship 600.

The aircraft were equipped with FLIR turrets on external pylons and Night-Sun searchlights. The S-76 and BO-105s were natural choices for SAUTT as the country has a long history of operating these types through its civilian National Helicopter Services Limited (NHSL).[84]

For Trinidad and Tobago to operate two separate air arms with no equipment compatibility makes no sense. It can be argued that the procurement of AW139s for the TTAG made little sense given NHSL's successful record with S-76s and BO-105s. This situation was exacerbated by a combination of economic hardship occasioned by a fall in the price of oil as well as the high maintenance costs of some of the assets.

Helicopter Assets – Growth and Decline

The Trinidad and Tobago Air Guard (TTAG) acquired four AW139 helicopters in the period 2010–2011. However, on 29 June 2017, in an unexpected decision, especially after investing over US$ 348 million in the acquisition of the helicopters and the training of personnel, the government of Trinidad and Tobago decided that it could no longer afford the annual maintenance costs of the helicopters amounting to some US$ 29 million.[85] Despite the fact that the TTAG's AW139 squadron had won awards for humanitarian assistance, and despite two previous administrations being committed to keeping the aircraft airworthy, the cost of maintaining the helicopters was deemed excessive.[86]

Since the TTAG remained entirely dependent on external contractors for the maintenance of the AW139s, they have been grounded since June 2017 in a closed hangar at the Ulric Cross Air Station at Piarco International Airport. To add to the ignominy, the government of Trinidad and Tobago was sued by Cobham, the company tasked with maintaining the AW139s, and failed to file a defence leading to the government having to pay US$ 10 million plus costs for a maintenance contract for helicopters that were unnecessarily grounded. In 2021, an attempt was made to reactivate one AW139 and the aircraft received certification from the country's Civil Aviation Authority, but none of the TTAG pilots are now current on type, most having left.

This decision has effectively meant the grounding of the TTAG as its two ageing C-26 aircraft are rarely operational and in dire need of replacement. The inability of Trinidad to create a local maintenance infrastructure has now come to haunt the TTAG and its existence may be doubtful as a separate establishment.

While the TTAG grapples to justify its existence, the National Operations Centre Air Division is facing severe challenges of its own. Flying hours have been savagely cut from over three hundred hours per year on average per pilot, to under one hundred with standing air surveillance patrols coming to a halt.[87] While at least part of the reduction in flying hours has been caused by curtailing the use of the NOC Air Division helicopters as VIP transports, the cuts to air patrols have proved to be detrimental to the unit's response time to incidents.

The efficiency of the helicopter fleet has been worsened by the failure to completely integrate Harris secure communications suites before the removal of earlier Motorola equipment leading to a virtual breakdown in real-time communication between the Air Division's helicopters and ground units. In addition, and somewhat inexplicably, the night-surveillance systems fitted to the NOC's AS.355 and two BO-105 helicopters are now non-operational and have been removed from the aircraft pending repairs which have not taken place to date – the equipment remaining in boxes at the Air Division's base in Central Trinidad.

An attempt to replace the NOC Air Division's ageing assets with a new fleet of four Bell 429 and one Bell 412EPI helicopters has become embroiled in a dispute with the government facing legal action over non-payment for both the helicopters and a special hangar for the aircraft.[88] Compounding these equipment issues was the non-payment of salaries to pilots which led to a 'sick-out' by aircrew, effectively grounding the Air Division briefly while the government sought to make the requisite payments.[89] The whole process culminated in the non-renewal of pilot contracts and the subsequent re-hiring of a few with the attendant disruption to services.

With the grounding of the AW139s, the NOC Air Division was transferred to the Trinidad and Tobago Air Guard. However, one of its S-76A++ helicopters has been

Table 23: Trinidad and Tobago's Air Assets

Platform family	Platform variant	Primary role (general)	Primary role (specific)	Estimated in service	First delivery date
Metro	C-26B	Maritime	Patrol	2	1999
One of the aircraft is equipped with Elta M-2022 radar and FLIR.					
AW139	AW139	Logistics	Utility	4 (withdrawn from use and grounded)	2011
AS.355F2	Ecureuil	Logistics	Utility	1	n/k
Sikorsky 76A	Sikorsky 76A	Logistics	Utility	1 grounded	n/k
BO-105CBS-4	BO-105CBS-4	Logistics	Utility	2	n/k

Austal Cape-class vessel TTS *Port of Spain*. (Austal)

grounded for over five years awaiting an autopilot, while a leased S-76D is now subject to legal proceedings after the government of Dr Keith Rowley refused to honour a lease executed by his opposition rival when she was Prime Minister. Of the remaining helicopters, only one AS.355 and one BO-105 are operational with another BO-105 being used as a spares source for the single operational machine of that type. Thus, from a fleet of ten helicopters in 2015, Trinidad has been reduced to two operational helicopters available for security operations, and these two lack surveillance equipment.

Conclusion

The TTDF is in dire need of a revamp, with reform and reorientation being necessary. However, with a very delicate internal security situation, the TTDF finds itself unable to carry out the reforms and reorientation that it knows to be necessary. Even the valid argument that a stronger TTCG which can seal off the import routes for weapons and narcotics and so rob the gangs of their financial resources and "muscle" has failed to make the necessary impact among decision makers. To them, the need to have the visible presence of the TTR in the fight against criminal gangs, owing to the inadequacies of the TTPS, takes priority and, as such, instituting reforms and reorienting the TTDF remains an aspiration that seems unlikely to be fulfilled.

The TTDF is a relatively large force, perhaps the largest in the Caribbean, but its efficacy has been crippled by an ad hoc procurement policy and a very casual, if not nonsensical approach to maintaining its assets. It also suffers from poor levels of accountability and lacks both the human and material resources to reach its full potential. It is replete with assets it cannot maintain and does not use efficiently. These shortcomings limit the utility of the force as a combat unit.

However, it should also be noted that this same force rose to the occasion when it was needed most desperately in 1990. Since the unfortunate events of 1970, the TTDF has shown itself to be fiercely committed to the Trinidadian Constitution and is a force with considerable potential to become more potent. While its challenges and limitations are well known, its positives of professionalism, an apolitical approach to its duties and its willingness to be an effective aid to the civil authority, stand it in good stead.

SELECT BIBLIOGRAPHY

Adkin, Mark, *Urgent Fury: The Battle for Grenada* (London: Leo Cooper, 1989)

Conway's All the World's Fighting Ships 1947-1995 (London, Conway Maritime Press: 1995)

Danns, G.K., *Domination and Power in Guyana* (New Brunswick: Transaction Books, 1982)

Disciplined Forces Commission Report (May 2004)

Furlonge-Kelly, E.T.V., *The Silent Victory* (Port of Spain: Golden Eagle, 1991)

Griffith, Ivelaw Lloyd, *Drugs and Security in the Caribbean: Sovereignty Under Siege* (Pennsylvania: Penn State Press: 1997)

Griffith, Ivelaw Lloyd, *The Quest for Security in the Caribbean: Problems and Promises in Subordinate States* (New York: M.E. Sharpe, 1993)

Hylton-Edwards, Stewart, *Lengthening Shadows: Birth and Revolt of the Trinidad Army* (Port of Spain: Inprint Caribbean: 1982)

Joint History Office of the Chairman of the Joint Chiefs of Staff *Operation Urgent Fury* (CreateSpace Independent Publishing Platform 2014)

Liverpool, Compton Hartley, *Foundation of the Guyana Defence Force: A Soldier of Valour Story* (AuthorHouse 2016; Kindle Edition)

O'Dowd, D.J., *Review of the Trinidad and Tobago Police Service* (Unpublished, May 1991)

Raines, Edgar F., *The Rucksack War* (Washington: Center for Military History, 2010)

Russell, Lee E. & Albert Mendez, M., *Grenada 1983* (London: Osprey, 1983)

Shah, Raffique, 'The People Have Absolved Me', in S. Ryan (ed.), Power: The Black Power Revolution 1970 (St Augustine: ISER, 1995)

Ryan, S., *The Muslimeen Grab for Power* (Port of Spain: Inprint, 1991)

Singh, C., *Guyana: Politics in a Plantation Society* (Stanford: Praeger Publ. 1988)

Trinidad and Tobago Parliament, *Report of the Commission of Enquiry into the 1990 attempted coup*, http://ttparliament.org/documents/rptcoe1990.pdf

Trinidad Under Siege (Daily Express 1990)

West Kingston Commission of Inquiry

NOTES

Chapter 1

1 Oscar Ramjeet, 'CARICOM Countries Will Speak With One Voice in Meetings With US And Canadian Leaders', *Caribbean Net News* (17 April 2009)http://www.caribbeannewsnow.com/caribnet/caricom/caricom.php?news_id=15757&start=440&category_id=39> accessed 8 Jul. 2016.

2 Sue Ann Wayow, 'Here's why T&T should pay attention to Brexit', *Trinidad Express* (24 June 2016), <http://www.trinidadexpress.com/20160624/business/heres-why-tt-should-pay-attention-to-brexit>, accessed 8 Jul. 2016.

3 'Countries and Regions – Caribbean', *European Commission*, <http://ec.europa.eu/trade/policy/countries-and-regions/regions/caribbean/>, accessed 8 Jul. 2021.

4 'Trinidad and Tobago PM hails Chinese dream', *China Daily Europe* (2 June 2013), <http://europe.chinadaily.com.cn/china/2013-06/02/content_16556395.htm>, accessed 1 Aug. 2016.

5 Robin Wigglesworth, 'Caribbean in crisis: Chequebook diplomacy', *Financial Times* (17 December 2013), <https://www.ft.com/content/7f7b0d8e-5ea8-11e3-8621-00144feabdc0>, accessed 1 Aug. 2016.

6 Robin Wigglesworth, 'Caribbean in crisis: Chequebook diplomacy'.

7 'About Us', *Regional Security System*, <https://www.rss.org.bb/about-us/>.

8 'Regional Security System', *Aeroflight*, <http://www.aeroflight.co.uk/ops/mil/regional-security-system.htm>.

9 Lee E. Russell & M. Albert Mendez, *Grenada 1983* (London: Osprey, 1983), pp.5–7 and pp.45–46.

10 Report on "Operation Carib" prepared by Colonel H.D. Maynard (23 August 1990).

11 Report on "Operation Carib".

12 Report on "Operation Carib".

13 Report on "Operation Carib".

14 Report on "Operation Carib".

15 Sanjay Badri-Maharaj, 'The Response of CARICOM Armed Forces to Hurricane Maria', *IDSA* (6 December 2017), <https://www.idsa.in/idsacomments/the-response-of-caricom-armed-forces-to-hurricane-maria_sbmaharaj_061217>

16 'CARICOM says Dominica getting strong regional support', *Stabroek News* (25 September 2017), <https://www.stabroeknews.com/2017/news/regional/09/25/caricom-says-dominica-getting-strong-regional-support/>, accessed 5 Dec. 2017.

17 'JDF disaster assistance team deployed to Dominica', *Jamaica Observer* (26 September 2017), <http://www.jamaicaobserver.com/latestnews/JDF_disaster_assistance_team_deployed_to_Dominica?profile=1228>, accessed 5 Dec. 2017.

18 'JDF DART in Dominica', *Jamaica Defence Force* (Facebook: 10 October 2017), <https://www.facebook.com/jdfsoldier/videos/10154798333461384/>, accessed 5 Dec. 2017.

19 Julia Rawlings-Bentham, 'A long road to recovery for Dominica', *Caribbean News Now* (28 September 2017), <http://wp.caribbeannewsnow.com/2017/09/28/long-road-recovery-dominica/>, accessed 5 Dec. 2017.

20 Sasha Harrinanan, 'Coast Guard provides swift aid to Dominica', *Trinidad Newsday* (22 September 2017), <http://newsday.co.tt/2017/09/22/coast-guard-provides-swift-aid-to-dominica/>, accessed 5 Dec. 2017.

21 'T&T Coast Guard vessel leaves for Dominica with relief items', *Loop TT* (5 October 2017) <http://www.looptt.com/content/tt-coast-guard-vessel-leaves-dominica-relief-items>, accessed 5 Dec. 2017.

22 'TTS NELSON II LEAVES FOR DOMINICA', *Trinidad and Tobago* (Facebook: 10 October 2017) <https://www.facebook.com/pg/Trinidad-Tobago-Coast-Guard-621931181194075/photos/?tab=album&album_id=1480087155378469>, accessed 5 Dec. 2017.

23 'HMBS Lawrence Major arrives in Dominica', *Royal Bahamas Defence Force* (29 October 2017), <http://rbdf.gov.bs/hmbs-lawrence-major-arrives-in-dominica/>, accessed 5 Dec. 2017.
24 Robin Wigglesworth, 'Caribbean in crisis: Chequebook diplomacy'.
25 'China to sell long range border patrol vessel to TT', *Trinidad Express* (25 February 2014), <https://trinidadexpress.com/news/china-to-provide-long-range-border-patrol-vessel-to-tt-247051311.html>, accessed 1 Aug. 2016.
26 Between 1979 and 1983, Grenada was a recipient of substantial military largesse from the former Soviet Union and Cuba.
27 Sanjay Badri-Maharaj, 'Coast Guards in the Western Hemisphere – The Dutch Connection', *IDSA* (27 September 2016), <https://idsa.in/idsacomments/coast-guards-western-hemisphere-the-dutch-connection_sbmaharaj_270916>.

Chapter 2

1 *Conway's All the World's Fighting Ships 1947-1995* (London: Conway Maritime Press, 1995), p.21.
2 'The Flamingo Incident', *Royal Bahamas Defence Force*, <https://rbdf.gov.bs/the-flamingo-incident/>.
3 'The Flamingo Incident', *Royal Bahamas Defence Force*.
4 'New Entry Training', *Royal Bahamas Defence Force*, <https://rbdf.gov.bs/new-entry-training/#1536606570863-c90e43ad-e2b0>.
5 'Police uneasy at move to call in RBDF in crime fight', *The Tribune* (24 February 2017), <http://www.tribune242.com/news/2017/feb/24/police-uneasy-move-call-rbdf-crime-fight/>, and 'Police, Defence Force Crime Fight Collaboration "A Shared Vision"', *The Tribune* (24 February 2017),<http://www.tribune242.com/news/2017/feb/24/police-defence-force-crime-fight-collaboration-sha/>.
6 'Commando Training', *RBDF*, <https://rbdf.gov.bs/commando-training/>.
7 'Two armoured vehicles are delivered as a gift from China', *The Tribune* (4 May 2017), <http://www.tribune242.com/news/2017/may/04/two-armoured-vehicles-are-delivered-gift-china/>.
8 Li Jiyao, 'China donates military equipment to the Bahamas', *China Mail* (12 September 2017)< http://eng.chinamil.com.cn/view/2017-09/12/content_7752376.htm>.
9 Sanjay Badri-Maharaj, 'The Royal Bahamas Defence Force: Poised for Capability Growth', *IDSA* (30 November 2016), <https://idsa.in/idsacomments/royal-bahamas-defence-force_sbmaharaj_301116>.
10 Sanjay Badri-Maharaj, 'The Royal Bahamas Defence Force: Poised for Capability Growth'
11 Sanjay Badri-Maharaj, 'The Royal Bahamas Defence Force: Poised for Capability Growth', *IDSA* (30 November 2016), <https://idsa.in/idsacomments/royal-bahamas-defence-force_sbmaharaj_301116>.
12 Sanjay Badri-Maharaj, 'The Royal Bahamas Defence Force: Poised for Capability Growth'
13 Sanjay Badri-Maharaj, 'The Royal Bahamas Defence Force: Poised for Capability Growth', *IDSA* (30 November 2016), <https://idsa.in/idsacomments/royal-bahamas-defence-force_sbmaharaj_301116>.
14 'Royal Bahamas Defence Force', *Aeroflight*, <http://www.aeroflight.co.uk/tag/royal-bahamas-defence-force>.
15 'RBDF Conducts Aerial Drone training', *The Nassau Guardian*, <http://www.thenassauguardian.com/news/66343-rbdf-conducts-aerial-drone-training-exercise->.
16 'Bahamas Unmanned Aerial Systems (BUAS) Solution', <https://www.bahamas.gov.bs/wps/wcm/connect/85264722-4318-4e82-9739-a5c16f9fd3c3/BAHAMAS+UNMANNED+AERIAL+SYSTEMS+SOLUTION+-+RFP+EXTENDED+TIME.pdf?MOD=AJPERES>.
17 'Role of the Royal Bahamas Defence Force Prior to a Hurricane', *Royal Bahamas Defence Force* (Facebook: 27 April 2020), <https://www.facebook.com/RBDFMIL/posts/the-role-of-the-royal-bahamas-defence-force-prior-to-a-hurricanethe-hurricane-se/2879252135443994/>.
18 Sanjay Badri-Maharaj, 'The Royal Bahamas Defence Force Faces Criticisms post-Hurricane Dorian', <https://informesinbandera.com/noticias/The_Royal_Bahamas_Defence_Force_Faces_Criticisms_post-Hurricane_Dorian_51e337bc68c557c2506b126aeb045992>.

Chapter 3

1 Ivelaw Lloyd Griffith, *The Quest for Security in the Caribbean: Problems and Promises in Subordinate States* (New York: M.E. Sharpe, 1993), pp.118–119.
2 Ivelaw Lloyd Griffith, *The Quest for Security in the Caribbean: Problems and Promises in Subordinate States* (New York: M.E. Sharpe, 1993) pp.118–119.
3 Ivelaw Lloyd Griffith, *The Quest for Security in the Caribbean*, pp.118–119.
4 'Interview with former arms dealer, mercenary leader', *The Weekend Nation* (3 February 1984), pp.16–17.
5 Dion E Phillips, 'The Creation, Structure and Training of the Barbados Defense Force', *Caribbean Studies*, 21:1/2 (1988), p.134.
6 'About the Barbados Coast Guard', *Barbados Defence Force* <https://www.bdfbarbados.com/the-barbados-coast-guard/>, accessed 8 Jul. 2021.
7 *Conway's All the World's Fighting Ships*, p.24.
8 'Barbados Defence Force', *Aeroflight*, <http://www.aeroflight.co.uk/ops/mil/barbados-defence-force.htm>.
9 Ivelaw Lloyd Griffith, *The Quest for Security in the Caribbean*, p.120.
10 '2 Guilty in New Orleans for plot on Dominica invasion', *The New York Times* (21 June 1981).
11 Mark Adkin, *Urgent Fury: The Battle for Grenada* (London: Leo Cooper, 1989), p.92.
12 Mark Adkin, *Urgent Fury*, pp.92–93.
13 Mark Adkin, *Urgent Fury*, pp.92–93.
14 Mark Adkin, *Urgent Fury*, pp.92–99.
15 Mark Adkin, *Urgent Fury*, pp.92–99.
16 Mark Adkin, *Urgent Fury*, p.93.
17 Mark Adkin, *Urgent Fury*, p.94.
18 Mark Adkin, *Urgent Fury*, pp.94–95.
19 Mark Adkin, *Urgent Fury*, pp.119–130.
20 Mark Adkin, *Urgent Fury*, pp.129–130.
21 Mark Adkin, *Urgent Fury*, p.219.
22 'The Caribbean Defence and Security', <http://www.resdal.org/ing/assets/atlas_2016_ing_08.pdf>.
23 Reserves include two rifle companies and a coast guard reserve – rifle companies do not exceed seventy personnel.
24 Rifles are now largely M16 variants but the British variant of the FN MAG GPMG is widely employed at section and platoon level.
25 Ivelaw Lloyd Griffith, *The Quest for Security in the Caribbean*, pp.118–123.
26 <https://www.barbadosparliament.com/.../44a64e31bf71ca9b9a02346b2b1fa3a6.pdf>, and Resolution Supplementary Estimates, No. 6, 2013–2014.
27 <https://www.barbadostoday.bb/2016/01/16/big-haul/>.
28 <https://www.barbadosparliament.com/.../44a64e31bf71ca9b9a02346b2b1fa3a6.pdf>.
29 'IAI ELTA Awarded Contract to Upgrade Barbados Coastal Surveillance Systems & Facilities', *Armada International* (7 May 2019), <https://armadainternational.com/2019/05/iai-elta-awarded-contract-to-upgrade-barbados-coastal-surveillance-systems-facilities/>.

Chapter 4

1 Overall total population, 'World Population Prospects: The 2019 Revision'
2 Guyana Census Compendium 2012, <https://statisticsguyana.gov.gy/wp-content/uploads/2019/11/Final_2012_Census_Compendium2.pdf>.
3 'Political and Economic History of Guyana', *SJSU*, <https://www.sjsu.edu/faculty/watkins/guyana.htm>.
4 'Political and Economic History of Guyana', *SJSU*, <https://www.sjsu.edu/faculty/watkins/guyana.htm>.
5 Janine Mendes-Franco, 'Appeal court says the answer to Guyana's election results lies in the recount', *Global Voices* (31 July 2020),

<https://globalvoices.org/2020/07/31/appeal-court-says-the-answer-to-guyanas-election-results-lies-in-the-recount/>.
6 D. Zwaagstra, 'Essequibo, the Territorial Dispute between Venezuela and Guyana', *Peace Palace Library* (8 January 2016), <https://www.peacepalacelibrary.nl/2016/01/essequibo-the-territorial-dispute-between-venezuela-and-guyana/>.
7 D. Zwaagstra, 'Essequibo, the Territorial Dispute between Venezuela and Guyana'.
8 'Gov't protests after Venezuela holds oil research boat', *Stabroek News* (12 October 2013), <https://www.stabroeknews.com/2013/10/12/news/guyana/govt-protests-after-venezuela-holds-oil-research-boat/>.
9 'Guyana says Exxon to begin offshore drilling, Venezuela irked', *Reuters*, accessed 8 Jun. 2015.
10 'Canciller guyanés convocará a embajadora venezolana', *El Universal* (8 June 2015).
11 'Venezuela navy confronts Exxon oil ship in Guyana border dispute', *Reuters* (23 December 2018).
12 'Guyana says two Venezuelan fighter jets flew over its airspace', *Reuters* (3 March 2021).
13 Guyana v Suriname, Award, ICGJ 370 (PCA 2007), 17 September 2007, Permanent Court of Arbitration [PCA]
14 'Guyana Army History', *Global Security.org*.
15 'Guyana Army History', *Global Security.org*.
16 'Guyana Army History', *Global Security.org*.
17 Compton Hartley Liverpool, *Foundation of the Guyana Defence Force: A Soldier of Valour Story* (AuthorHouse 2016; Kindle edition), p.40.
18 Compton Hartley Liverpool, *Foundation of the Guyana Defence Force*, p.102.
19 'History of the 21 Artillery Company', defunct Guyana Defence Force website (author's notes).
20 'History of the 21 Artillery Company'.
21 'History of the 21 Artillery Company'.
22 'History of the 21 Artillery Company'.
23 'History of the 21 Artillery Company'.
24 'Guyana Defence Force', *Aeroflight*, <http://www.aeroflight.co.uk/ops/mil/guyana-defence-force.htm>.
25 'Guyana Defence Force', *Aeroflight*.
26 'All-Time Aircraft Used List Guyana Defence Force', *Aeroflight*, <http://www.aeroflight.co.uk/user/every/guyana-df-all-time-aircraft-list.htm>.
27 Compton Hartley Liverpool, *Foundation of the Guyana Defence Force*, pp.181–184.
28 Compton Hartley Liverpool, *Foundation of the Guyana Defence Force*, pp.182–184.
29 Compton Hartley Liverpool, *Foundation of the Guyana Defence Force*, pp.182–184.
30 Compton Hartley Liverpool, *Foundation of the Guyana Defence Force*, pp.182–184.
31 Compton Hartley Liverpool, *Foundation of the Guyana Defence Force*, pp.182–184.
32 Compton Hartley Liverpool, *Foundation of the Guyana Defence Force*, pp.182–184.
33 Compton Hartley Liverpool, *Foundation of the Guyana Defence Force*, pp.182–184.
34 Compton Hartley Liverpool, *Foundation of the Guyana Defence Force*, pp.182–184.
35 'Amerindian News', *Georgetown*, 2:3 (15 May 1968).
36 Manuel Felipe Sierra, 'Guyana: from Rupununi to the Hague', *Eneltapete* (7 April 2020), <https://www.eneltapete.com/historia/1407/guyana-de-rupununi-a-la-haya>.
37 D. Granger, 'The Rupununi Rebellion, 1969', *Stabroek News* (18 January 2009), <https://www.stabroeknews.com/2009/01/18/features/the-rupununi-rebellion-1969/>.
38 D. Granger, 'The Defence of the New River, 1967-1969', *Stabroek News* (15 February 2009), <https://www.stabroeknews.com/2009/02/15/features/the-defence-of-the-new-river-1967-1969/>.
39 D. Granger, 'The Defence of the New River, 1967-1969'.
40 D. Granger, 'The Defence of the New River, 1967-1969'.
41 P. Jardim, 'Guyana Defends Itself', *Guyana Then and Now*, <https://guyanathenandnow.wordpress.com/british-guiana-airways-limited/>.
42 P. Jardim, 'Guyana Defends Itself'.
43 Michael Chan-A-Sue, 'The Guns of August', *Guyana Loop*, <https://guyana.hoop.la/topic/the-guns-of-august>.
44 D. Granger, 'The Defence of the New River, 1967-1969'.
45 G.K. Danns, *Domination and Power in Guyana* (New Brunswick: Transaction Books, 1982), pp.117–118.
46 G.K. Danns, *Domination and Power*, pp.119–120.
47 *Report of the British Guiana Commission of Inquiry*, p.49.
48 PPP newspaper, *The Mirror* (10 June 1973).
49 G.K. Danns, *Domination and Power*, pp.120–122.
50 G.K. Danns, *Domination and Power*, pp.58–66.
51 C. Singh, *Guyana: Politics in a Plantation Society* (Stanford: Praeger Publ. 1988), pp.76–77.
52 C. Singh, *Guyana: Politics in a Plantation Society*, pp.70–85.
53 G.K. Danns, *Domination and Power*, pp.122–125.
54 G.K. Danns, *Domination and Power*, pp.122–125.
55 G.K. Danns, *Domination and Power*, pp.122–125.
56 'A policeman died in 1973', *Kaiteur News* (1 April 2015), <https://www.kaieteurnewsonline.com/2015/04/01/a-policeman-died-in-1973/>.
57 C. Singh, *Guyana: Politics in a Plantation Society*, pp.76–105.
58 Unofficial pdf copy of the Disciplined Forces Commission Report, May 2004 (obtained by the author), p.196.
59 Unofficial pdf copy of the Disciplined Forces Commission Report, p.89.
60 'GDF pledges "loyalty" to "democratically elected" government, Commander-in-Chief', *Demerara Waves* (3 August 2020), <https://demerarawaves.com/2020/08/03/gdf-pledges-loyalty-to-democratically-elected-government-commander-in-chief/>.
61 'Guyana Defence Force', *Global Security.org*.
62 '1,608 persons recruited to Guyana People's Militia – Min. Harmon', *Department of Public Information* (19 July 2018).
63 'Guyana Army', *Global Security.org*.
64 'Guyana Army', *Global Security.org*.
65 'GDF Skyvans arrive', *Guyana Chronicle* (29 June 2019), <https://guyanachronicle.com/2019/06/29/gdf-skyvans-arrive>.
66 'Guyana Defence Force Skyvans arrive', *Demerara Waves* (28 June 2019), <https://demerarawaves.com/2019/06/28/guyana-defence-force-skyvans-arrive/>.
67 G. Reim, 'Bell approved to sell two 412EPI and two 429 helicopters to Guyana', *Flight Global* (30 October 2020), <https://www.flightglobal.com/helicopters/bell-approved-to-sell-two-412epi-and-two-429-helicopters-to-guyana/140906.article>.
68 Julieta Pelcastre, 'Guyana Receives Bell 412 Helicopter to Improve Air Security', *Dialogo Americas* (26 April 2021), <https://dialogo-americas.com/articles/guyana-receives-bell-412-helicopter-to-improve-air-security/>.
69 'Acquisition of Bell 412EPI helicopter boosts Guyana's security – Army Chief", *iNews Guyana* (14 March 2021), <https://www.inewsguyana.com/acquisition-of-bell-412epi-helicopter-boosts-guyanas-security-army-chief/>.
70 'GDF Coast Guard to get more vessels this year', *Demerara Waves* (13 March 2021), <https://demerarawaves.com/2021/03/13/gdf-coast-guard-to-get-more-vessels-this-year/>.

Chapter 5

1 *Jamaica Population 2021, World Population Review* <https://worldpopulationreview.com/countries/jamaica-population>.
2 'Mission', *Jamaica Defence Force*, <https://www.jdfweb.com/mission/>.
3 'More Police Welcome', *The Jamaica Gleaner* (9 September 2019), <https://jamaica-gleaner.com/article/commentary/20190909/editorial-more-police-welcome>.
4 'History', *Jamaica Defence Force*, <https://www.jdfweb.com/history/>.
5 'History', *Jamaica Defence Force*.

6 'History', *Jamaica Defence Force.*
7 The West Indies Federation, *CARICOM*, <https://caricom.org/the-west-indies-federation/>.
8 Humphrey Metzgen and John Graham, *Caribbean Wars Untold: A Salute to the British West Indies* (2007), ISBN 9766402035, ISBN 9789766402037.
9 Terry Lacey, *Violence and politics in Jamaica 1960-1970: internal security in developing country*, 1977, ISBN 0719006333, ISBN 9780719006333, p.107.
10 Terry Lacey, *Violence and politics in Jamaica 1960-1970*, p.107
11 Terry Lacey, *Violence and politics in Jamaica 1960-1970*, pp.105–115.
12 'History', *Jamaica Defence Force.*
13 'Jamaica Regiment', *Global Security.org*, <https://www.globalsecurity.org/military/world/caribbean/jm-regiment.htm>.
14 'Jamaica Regiment', *Global Security.*
15 'Jamaica Regiment', *Global Security.*
16 'Jamaica Regiment', G*lobal Security.*
17 'Jamaica Regiment', *Global Security.*
18 'Jamaica Regiment', *Global Security.*
19 'JDF to Acquire New Fleet of Armoured Vehicles', *Jamaica Information Service* (3 December 2013), <https://jis.gov.jm/jdf-acquire-new-fleet-armoured-vehicles/>.
20 'Jamaica Defence Force', *Aeroflight*, <http://www.aeroflight.co.uk/ops/mil/jamaican-defence-force.htm>.
21 'Jamaica Defence Force', *Aeroflight.*
22 'Jamaica Defence Force', *Aeroflight.*
23 'Jamaica Defence Force', *Aeroflight.*
24 'All-Time Aircraft Used List Jamaican Defence Force', *Aeroflight*, <http://www.aeroflight.co.uk/user/every/jamaica-df-all-time-aircraft-used-listing.htm>.
25 '1st District Jamaica Defence Force Coast Guard', *Jamaica Defence Force*, <https://www.jdfweb.com/1st-dist-jdf-coast-guard/>.
26 '1st District Jamaica Defence Force Coast Guard', *Jamaica Defence Force.*
27 *Conway's All the World's Fighting Ships*, p.219.
28 Ivelaw Lloyd Griffith, *The Quest for Security in the Caribbean*, p.136.
29 Joint History Office of the Chairman of the Joint Chiefs of Staff, *Operation Urgent Fury* (CreateSpace Independent Publishing Platform 2014), p.36.
30 Edgar F. Raines, *The Rucksack War* (Washington: Center for Military History, 2010), p.356.
31 *West Kingston Commission of Inquiry* (Government of Jamaica, 2014), pp.36–39.
32 *West Kingston Commission of Inquiry*, pp.41–42.
33 *West Kingston Commission of Inquiry*, pp.42–43.
34 *West Kingston Commission of Inquiry*, p.44.
35 *West Kingston Commission of Inquiry*, pp.45–48.
36 *West Kingston Commission of Inquiry*, pp.60–62.
37 *West Kingston Commission of Inquiry*, p.61.
38 *West Kingston Commission of Inquiry*, p.65.
39 *West Kingston Commission of Inquiry*, p.73.
40 *West Kingston Commission of Inquiry*, p.74.
41 *West Kingston Commission of Inquiry*, pp.76–77.
42 *West Kingston Commission of Inquiry*, p.78.
43 *West Kingston Commission of Inquiry*, p.80.
44 *West Kingston Commission of Inquiry*, pp.156–157.
45 *West Kingston Commission of Inquiry*, p.330, and pp.334–335.
46 *West Kingston Commission of Inquiry*, p.433.
47 *West Kingston Commission of Inquiry*, p.15.
48 'Organization', *Jamaica Defence Force*, <https://www.jdfweb.com/organization/>.
49 Jamaica Defence Force – Jamaica Regiment', *Jamaica Defence Force*, <https://www.jdfweb.com/jamaica-regiment/>.
50 Jamaica Defence Force – Jamaica Regiment', *Jamaica Defence Force*, <https://www.jdfweb.com/jamaica-regiment/>.
51 'National Reserves called out amid crime wave', *Jamaica* Star (23 September 2016), <http://jamaica-star.com/article/20160923/national-reserves-called-out-amid-crime-wave>.
52 'Jamaica Regiment', *Jamaica Defence Force*, <https://www.jdfweb.com/1st-bn-the-jamaica-regiment/>.
53 Sanjay Badri-Maharaj, 'The Jamaica Defence Force – Balancing Priorities with Resources', *IDSA*, <https://idsa.in/idsacomments/the-jamaica-defence-force_sbmaharaj_091216>.
54 'Combat Support Battalion', *Jamaica Defence Force*, <https://www.jdfweb.com/combat-support-bn/>.
55 'Support Brigade', *Jamaica Defence Force*, <https://www.jdfweb.com/support-brigade/>.
56 '1 Engineer Regiment (JDF)', *Jamaica Defence Force*, <https://www.jdfweb.com/1-engineer-regiment-jdf/>.
57 'National Reserve', *Jamaica Defence Force*, <https://www.jdfweb.com/jamaica-national-reserve/>.
58 'Maritime, Air and Cyber Command', *Jamaica Defence Force*, <https://www.jdfweb.com/maritime-air-and-cyber-command/>.
59 John Duke & Lloyd Horrigan, *Vertical Mag* (10 September 2020), <https://verticalmag.com/features/pilots-of-the-caribbean-the-jamaica-defense-force-airs-out-its-bell-429s/>.
60 John Duke & Lloyd Horrigan, *Vertical Mag.*
61 John Duke & Lloyd Horrigan, *Vertical Mag.*
62 John Duke & Lloyd Horrigan, *Vertical Mag.*
63 'Bell announces sale of six Bell 505s to Jamaica Defence Force', *Vertical Mag* (8 February 2021), <https://verticalmag.com/press-releases/bell-announces-sale-bell-505-jamaica-defence-force/>.
64 'JDF Acquires New Surveillance Aircraft', *Jamaica Information Service* (16 November 2018), <https://jis.gov.jm/jdf-acquires-new-surveillance-aircraft/>.
65 'Jamaica acquires four offshore patrol vehicles, two maritime aircraft', *Stabroek News* (26 June 2020), <https://www.stabroeknews.com/2020/06/26/news/regional/jamaica/jamaica-acquires-four-offshore-patrol-vehicles-two-maritime-aircraft/>.
66 'Decommissioning ceremony for Her Majesty Jamaica Ship Paul Bogle (P8)', *Jamaica Defence Force*, <https://www.jdfweb.com/the-official-handing-over-and-renaming-ceremony/>.
67 'Jamaica Defence Force Coast Guard (JDF CG)', *Global Security*, <https://www.globalsecurity.org/military/world/caribbean/jm-coast-guard.htm>.
68 'JDF now boasts Caribbean's largest maritime presence', *Jamaica Gleaner* (29 October 2017), <https://jamaica-gleaner.com/article/auto/20171029/jdf-now-boasts-caribbeans-largest-maritime-presence>.
69 'Facilitating collaborative commonality in the Caribbean with patrol boats', *Damen Magazine* (January 2021), <https://www.damen.com/en/magazines/2021/01/increasing-caribbean-capabilities-offshore-patrol-vessels>.
70 'Facilitating collaborative commonality in the Caribbean with patrol boats'.
71 'Facilitating collaborative commonality in the Caribbean with patrol boats'.
72 Mateo Natalucci, 'Jamaica orders Thales's coastal surveillance system', *Janes.com*, <https://www.janes.com/defence-news/news-detail/jamaica-orders-thaless-coastal-surveillance-system>.

Chapter 6

1 Trinidad and Tobago Literacy, <http://www.indexmundi.com/trinidad_and_tobago/literacy.html>.
2 'IMF World Economic Outlook Data', *International Monetary Fund*, <http://www.imf.org/external/pubs/ft/weo/2015/01/weodata/weorept.aspx?sy=2014&ey=2019&scsm=1&ssd=1&sort=country&ds=.&br= 1&pr1.x=73&pr1.y=10&c=369&s=NGDPD 2CNGDPDPC 2CPPPGDP 2CPPPPC&grp=0&a>.
3 'Trinidad and Tobago Demographic Report 2011', *Central Statistical Office*, <http://cso.planning.gov.tt/sites/default/files/content/images/census/TRINIDAD%20AND%20TOBAGO%202011%20Demographic%20Report.pdfhttp://www.trinidadexpress.com/news/Census__Mixed_population_on_the_rise-191944721.html>, p.15.
4 'Trinidad and Tobago Demographic Report 2011', *Central Statistical Office*, pp.17–18.

5 Ivelaw Lloyd Griffith, *Drugs and Security in the Caribbean: Sovereignty Under Siege* (Pennsylvania: Penn State Press, 1997), pp.47–48.
6 Ivelaw Lloyd Griffith, *Drugs and Security in the Caribbean*, p.69.
7 Ivelaw Lloyd Griffith, *Drugs and Security in the Caribbean*, p.84.
8 Ivelaw Lloyd Griffith, *Drugs and Security in the Caribbean*, pp.119–120.
9 '89 Trinis join Isis fighters', *Trinidad Guardian* (16 November 2016), <http://www.guardian.co.tt/news/2015-11-16/89-trinis-join-isis-fighters>.
10 G. Alexander, 'Serious threat to T&T', *Trinidad Guardian* (15 April 2016), <http://www.guardian.co.tt/news/2016-04-15/serious-threat-tt>.
11 G. Alexander, 'Govt to meet Muslims on Isis', *Trinidad Guardian* (7 August 2016), <http://www.guardian.co.tt/news/2016-08-07/govt-meet-muslims-isis>.
12 C. Kissoon, 'Trini children in ISIS recruitment video', *Trinidad Express* (6 November 2016) <http://www.trinidadexpress.com/20151106/news/trini-children-in-isis-recruitment-video>.
13 Ivelaw Lloyd Griffith, *The Quest for Security in the Caribbean*, p.109.
14 Stewart Hylton Edwards, *Lengthening Shadows: Birth and Revolt of the Trinidad Army* (Port of Spain: Inprint Caribbean, 1982), p.22.
15 Stewart Hylton Edwards, *Lengthening Shadows*, p.33.
16 Stewart Hylton Edwards, *Lengthening Shadows*, p.30.
17 Stewart Hylton Edwards, *Lengthening Shadows*, p.31.
18 Stewart Hylton Edwards, *Lengthening Shadows*, p.100.
19 Raffique Shah, 'Takeover of Teteron ...one shot was all it took', <http://www.trinicenter.com/1970/Blackpower5.htm>.
20 Raffique Shah, 'Takeover of Teteron ...one shot was all it took'.
21 Raffique Shah, 'Takeover of Teteron ...one shot was all it took'.
22 Raffique Shah, 'Takeover of Teteron ...one shot was all it took'.
23 Raffique Shah, 'Panic in the city', <http://www.trinicenter.com/1970/Blackpower6.htm>.
24 Raffique Shah, 'The People Have Absolved Me', in S. Ryan (ed.), *Power: The Black Power Revolution 1970* (St Augustine: ISER, 1995), p.482.
25 Raffique Shah, 'Panic in the city'.
26 Raffique Shah, 'Battle for the hillside', <http://www.trinicenter.com/1970/Blackpower7.htm>.
27 Raffique Shah, 'Battle for the hillside'.
28 Raffique Shah, 'Battle for the hillside'.
29 Raffique Shah, 'Battle for the hillside'.
30 Raffique Shah, 'Weapons down, amnesty for all', <http://www.trinicenter.com/1970/Blackpower8.htm>.
31 For a fuller account of the events described here, see Sanjay Badri-Maharaj, *Trinidad 1990: The Caribbean's Islamist Insurrection* (Warwick: Helion & Company, 2020)
32 Author's research – visual identification of both weapons and equipment.
33 Author's research – visual identification of both weapons and equipment.
34 Sanjay Badri-Maharaj, 'Rebuilding the Trinidad and Tobago Coast Guard', *Institute for Defence Studies and Analyses* (26 August 2016), <https://idsa.in/idsacomments/rebuilding-the-trinidad-and-tobago-coast-guard_sbmaharaj_260816>.
35 Sanjay Badri-Maharaj, 'Rebuilding the Trinidad and Tobago Coast Guard', *Institute for Defence Studies and Analyses* (26 August 2016), <https://idsa.in/idsacomments/rebuilding-the-trinidad-and-tobago-coast-guard_sbmaharaj_260816>.
36 Sanjay Badri-Maharaj, 'Rebuilding the Trinidad and Tobago Coast Guard'.
37 D.J. O'Dowd, *Review of the Trinidad and Tobago Police Service* (Unpublished, May 1991), Chapter 11, para 3.5, subpara 3.1.1.
38 Sanjay Badri-Maharaj, 'Trinidad and Tobago – An Emerging Security Scenario', *Air Combat Information Group* (29 December 2011), <https://web.archive.org/web/20120723075914/http://www.acig.info/CMS/index.php?option=com_content&task=view&id=258&Itemid=47>.
39 Trinidad and Tobago Parliament, *Report of the Commission of Enquiry into the 1990 attempted coup*, <http://ttparliament.org/documents/rptcoe1990.pdf>.
40 Trinidad and Tobago Parliament, *Report of the Commission of Enquiry into the 1990 attempted coup*.
41 Trinidad and Tobago Parliament, *Report of the Commission of Enquiry into the 1990 attempted coup*, pp.258–259.
42 Trinidad and Tobago Parliament, *Report of the Commission of Enquiry into the 1990 attempted coup*, pp.56–57.
43 E.T.V. Furlonge-Kelly, *The Silent Victory* (Port of Spain: Golden Eagle, 1991), p.33.
44 Trinidad and Tobago Parliament, *Report of the Commission of Enquiry into the 1990 attempted coup*, pp.251–254.
45 Trinidad and Tobago Parliament, *Report of the Commission of Enquiry into the 1990 attempted coup*, pp.251–254.
46 Trinidad and Tobago Parliament, *Report of the Commission of Enquiry into the 1990 attempted coup*, pp.385–390.
47 Trinidad and Tobago Parliament, *Report of the Commission of Enquiry into the 1990 attempted coup*, pp.385–386.
48 Trinidad and Tobago Parliament, *Report of the Commission of Enquiry into the 1990 attempted coup*, p.335.
49 Trinidad and Tobago Parliament, *Report of the Commission of Enquiry into the 1990 attempted coup*, pp.265–266.
50 Trinidad and Tobago Parliament, *Report of the Commission of Enquiry into the 1990 attempted coup*, pp.274–282.
51 Trinidad and Tobago Parliament, *Report of the Commission of Enquiry into the 1990 attempted coup*, p.246.
52 Trinidad and Tobago Parliament, *Report of the Commission of Enquiry into the 1990 attempted coup*, p.148.
53 Interview with Major General Ralph Brown (22 September 1999).
54 *Report to the Minister of Justice and National Security*, prepared by Joseph Theodore (23 August 1990).
55 S. Ryan, *The Muslimeen Grab for Power* (Port of Spain: Inprint, 1991), p.158.
56 Trinidad and Tobago Parliament, *Report of the Commission of Enquiry into the 1990 attempted coup*, p.150.
57 Trinidad and Tobago Parliament, *Report of the Commission of Enquiry into the 1990 attempted coup*, pp.877–878.
58 Trinidad and Tobago Parliament, *Report of the Commission of Enquiry into the 1990 attempted coup*, p.888.
59 Trinidad and Tobago Parliament, *Report of the Commission of Enquiry into the 1990 attempted coup*, p.889.
60 Trinidad and Tobago Parliament, *Report of the Commission of Enquiry into the 1990 attempted coup*, p.889.
61 Trinidad and Tobago Parliament, *Report of the Commission of Enquiry into the 1990 attempted coup*, pp.880–895.
62 Trinidad and Tobago Parliament, *Report of the Commission of Enquiry into the 1990 attempted coup*, pp.888–891.
63 Trinidad and Tobago Parliament, *Report of the Commission of Enquiry into the 1990 attempted coup*, pp.888–891.
64 Trinidad and Tobago Parliament, *Report of the Commission of Enquiry into the 1990 attempted coup*, pp.888–891.
65 Trinidad and Tobago Parliament, *Report of the Commission of Enquiry into the 1990 attempted coup*, pp.154–157.
66 Trinidad and Tobago Parliament, *Report of the Commission of Enquiry into the 1990 attempted coup*, pp.154–157.
67 Trinidad and Tobago Parliament, *Report of the Commission of Enquiry into the 1990 attempted coup*, pp.154–157.
68 Trinidad and Tobago Parliament, *Report of the Commission of Enquiry into the 1990 attempted coup*, pp.154–157.
69 Trinidad and Tobago Parliament, *Report of the Commission of Enquiry into the 1990 attempted coup*, pp.154–157.
70 Trinidad and Tobago Parliament, *Report of the Commission of Enquiry into the 1990 attempted coup*, pp.154–157.
71 Trinidad and Tobago Parliament, *Report of the Commission of Enquiry into the 1990 attempted coup*, p.7.
72 Sanjay Badri-Maharaj, 'Rebuilding the Trinidad and Tobago Coast Guard', *IDSA* (26 August 2016), <http://idsa.in/idsacomments/rebuilding-the-trinidad-and-tobago-coast-guard_sbmaharaj_260816>.

73 Sanjay Badri-Maharaj, 'Trinidad and Tobago Coast Guard and the Australian Connection', *IDSA* (8 June 2018), <https://www.idsa.in/idsacomments/trinidad-and-tobago-coast-guard-and-australian_sbmaharaj-080619>.

74 Sanjay Badri-Maharaj 'How the SPa was Chosen – The Trinidad and Tobago Coast Guard's DAMEN SPa 5009 fleet', *Chuck Hill's CG Blog* (18 March 2018), <https://chuckhillscgblog.net/2018/03/18/how-the-spa-was-chosen-the-trinidad-and-tobago-coast-guards-damen-spa-5009-fleet/>.

75 Sanjay Badri-Maharaj 'How the SPa was Chosen – The Trinidad and Tobago Coast Guard's DAMEN SPa 5009 fleet', *Chuck Hill's CG Blog* (18 March 2018), <https://chuckhillscgblog.net/2018/03/18/how-the-spa-was-chosen-the-trinidad-and-tobago-coast-guards-damen-spa-5009-fleet/>.

76 Sanjay Badri-Maharaj 'How the SPa was Chosen – The Trinidad and Tobago Coast Guard's DAMEN SPa 5009 fleet', *Chuck Hill's CG Blog* (18 March 2018), <https://chuckhillscgblog.net/2018/03/18/how-the-spa-was-chosen-the-trinidad-and-tobago-coast-guards-damen-spa-5009-fleet/>.

77 Sanjay Badri-Maharaj, 'Trinidad and Tobago's Maritime Security: Myths and Reality', *The Kootneeti* (29 July 2020), <https://thekootneeti.in/2020/07/29/trinidad-and-tobagos-maritime-security-myths-and-reality/>.

78 Sanjay Badri-Maharaj, 'Trinidad and Tobago's Maritime Security: Myths and Reality', *The Kootneeti* (29 July 2020), <https://thekootneeti.in/2020/07/29/trinidad-and-tobagos-maritime-security-myths-and-reality/>.

79 'Austal Australia launches first of two cape-class patrol boats for Trinidad and Tobago coast guard', *Austal* (4 December 2020), <https://www.austal.com/news/austal-australia-launches-first-two-cape-class-patrol-boats-trinidad-and-tobago-coast-guard>.

80 Sanjay Badri-Maharaj, 'Trinidad and Tobago's Air Arms: Inefficient Duplication of Effort', *IDSA* (21 September 2016), <http://idsa.in/idsacomments/trinidad-and-tobagos-air-arms_sbmaharaj_210916>.

81 Sanjay Badri-Maharaj, 'Trinidad and Tobago – An Emerging Security Scenario'.

82 Sanjay Badri-Maharaj, 'Trinidad and Tobago – An Emerging Security Scenario'.

83 Sanjay Badri-Maharaj, 'Trinidad and Tobago's Air Arms: Inefficient Duplication of Effort'.

84 Sanjay Badri-Maharaj, 'Trinidad and Tobago's Air Arms: Inefficient Duplication of Effort'.

85 Darlisha Ghouralal, 'Helicopters grounded: $200m maintenance too costly', *Loop TT* (30 June 2017), <http://www.looptt.com/content/helicopters-grounded-200m-maintenance-too-costly>.

86 'Trinidad and Tobago Air Guard Helicopters grounded as government refuses $28.75 million maintenance obligation', *Helicopter News Wire* (13 July 2017), <http://helicopternewswire.com/trinidad-tobago-air-guard-helicopters-grounded-government-refuses-28-75-million-maintenance-obligation>, accessed 5 April 2018.

87 Telephone conversation with NOC Air Division Senior Pilot, 24 November 2017.

88 Anna Ramdass, 'Govt faces legal action over contract for helicopters, hangar', *Trinidad Express* (13 October 2017), <https://www.trinidadexpress.com/news/local/govt-faces-legal-action-over-contract-for-helicopters-hangar/article_305c4f1f-25af-54d9-9b13-997ba36b881c.html>.

89 Khamal Georges, 'Pay protest at Air Division grounds security copters', *Trinidad Guardian* (27 February 2018), <http://www.guardian.co.tt/news/2018-02-26/pay-protest-air-division-grounds-security-copters>.

ABOUT THE AUTHOR

Sanjay Badri-Maharaj, from Trinidad and Tobago, received his MA and PhD from the epartment of War Studies, Kings College London. His thesis was on India's Nuclear Weapons Program. He has written and published extensively, including *The Armageddon Factor: Nuclear Weapons in the India-Pakistan Context* (2000) and *Indian Nuclear Strategy: Confronting the Potential Nuclear Threat from both Pakistan and China* (2018), as well as *Kargil 1999, Trinidad 1990, Operation Meghdoot* and *Nuclear India* for Helion's @War series. He has served as a consultant to the Ministry of National Security in Trinidad and was a visiting International Fellow at the Institute for Defence Studies and Analyses, New Delhi.